CHRISTMAS

RECIPES

Creative Christmas Recipe Ideas for Your Friends and Family

(The Best Christmas Dessert Recipes)

Brian Anderson

Published by Alex Howard

© Brian Anderson

All Rights Reserved

Christmas Recipes: Creative Christmas Recipe Ideas for Your Friends and Family (The Best Christmas Dessert Recipes)

ISBN 978-1-989891-97-1

All rights reserved. No part of this guide may be reproduced in any form without permission in writing from the publisher except in the case of brief quotations embodied in critical articles or reviews.

Legal & Disclaimer

The information contained in this book is not designed to replace or take the place of any form of medicine or professional medical advice. The information in this book has been provided for educational and entertainment purposes only.

The information contained in this book has been compiled from sources deemed reliable, and it is accurate to the best of the Author's knowledge; however, the Author cannot guarantee its accuracy and validity and cannot be held liable for any errors or omissions. Changes are periodically made to this book. You must consult your doctor or get professional medical advice before using any of the suggested remedies, techniques, or information in this book.

Table of contents

PART 1 1

INTRODUCTION 2

    DELICIOUS CHRISTMAS RECIPES 4

DRINKS 4

    HOLIDAY CITRUS PUNCH 4
    CHRISTMAS COCKTAIL 5
    CINNAMON SPICED COFFEE 6
    CLASSIC HOLIDAY EGGNOG 7
    CLOVE AND CINNAMON BREW 8

STARTERS 9

    TOMATO AND BASIL MOZZARELLA SKEWERS 9
    SAUSAGE AND CHEESE BALLS 10
    BEEFY CHEESE CREAM BALL 11
    BAKED CHEDDAR AND CREAM CHEESE DIP 12
    THREE CHEESE CHRISTMAS HOLIDAY TREE 13
    BLUE CHEESE AND WALNUT CRISPS 16
    PIMENTO FINGER SANDWICHES 17
    BAKED SPINACH AND CHEESE DIP 18

SALADS AND SIDE DISHES 20

    CREAMY CHRISTMAS CRANBERRY SLAW 20
    RED AND GREEN CHRISTMAS VEGGIES 21
    SPINACH AND CRANBERRY SALAD 23
    CREAMY CREOLE CORN 24
    CREAMY ONIONS AND HERBS 25

ENTREES 27

    HOLIDAY CHICKEN A LA KING 27

CHRISTMAS PORK LOIN 28
ROMANO CRUSTED RIB ROAST 29
YULE-TIME HOLIDAY HAM 31
HERB CRUSTED SALMON PATTIES 32
HONEY GLAZED HOLIDAY HAM 32
CLASSIC CHRISTMAS TURKEY 34

DESSERTS 36

PISTACHIO CREAM LAYER CAKE 36
MARSHMALLOW AND PECAN BOWLS 37
CHRISTMAS CRISPIES 38
CHRISTMAS PUDDING CUPS 39
HOLIDAY TOFFEE CRUNCH 41

PART 2 43

INTRODUCTION 44

CHAPTER 1: WHAT POTENTIAL CAUSES AND WHO USUALLY GET DIABETES 52

CHAPTER 2: DIABETES DIETING TIPS AND WHAT FOODS TO EAT 56

CHAPTER 3: BEST HEALTH SUPPLEMENTS FOR DIABETES 63

CHAPTER 4: BREAKFAST RECIPES 67

DENVER OMELET 67
SPINACH AND SWISS QUICHE 69
HAM ROLLUPS 71
HUEVOS RANCHEROS 73
SAUSAGE EGG MUFFINS 75
JUNIOR MINT SHAKE 76

CHAPTER 5: MAIN DISH RECIPES 78

SMOTHERED PAN SEARED SALMON 78
KETO FRIENDLY CHILI 80
ZUCCHINI CASSEROLE 81

Parmesan Halibut	84
Tilapia and Broccoli	85
Steak Salad with Asian Spice	87
Hangar Steak	89
2 tablespoons of soy sauce Italian Meatballs	91
Healthy Kale Chicken Caesar Salad	93
Oven Roasted Broccoli with Parmesan Cheese and Garlic	95
Simple Salisbury Steak	97
Classic Prime Rib	99
Chicken Chow Mein Stir Fry	100
Kabobs with Peanut Curry Sauce	103
Alfredo with Scallop and Asparagus	104
Chicken Piccata	106
Indian Chicken Curry	108
No Bake Cheesecake	110
Cauliflower Soup	112
Mulled Wine	114
Gambas « verrine »	115
Smoked Salmon Canapés	116
Mushrooms with Foie Gras	117
A Spoonful of Crab	118
Blinis with Ham and Mozzarella	119
Leeks and Scallops Blinis	121
Pear and Foie Gras Verrine	122
Fig Chutney	123
Goat Cheese and Fig Toast	124
Skewered Scallops with Bacon, Creamed Vegetables Baked in Parchment Parcels	126
Scallop Cassolette	128
Warm Oysters with Champagne Sabayon	130
Oyster Tartar with Prawns	131
Scallop and Fish Terrine	133

DUCK TERRINE WITH NUTS	135
STUFFED GUINEA FOWL	137
GUINEA FOWL STUFFED WITH PRUNES	139
QUAIL STUFFED WITH MORELS	140
QUAILS WITH CHESTNUTS	141
PIGEONS WITH BACON BITS AND MUSHROOMS	143
PHEASANT IN CHAMPAGNE	144
PARTRIDGE WITH CEPS AND MUSCAT	145
CHRISTMAS POT ROAST	147
ROAST CAPON	149
TRUFFLED CAPON POACHED IN CHAMPAGNE	151
CAPON IN VIN DE PAILLE	153
TURKEY STUFFED WITH CHESTNUTS	155
ROASTED DUCK BREASTS WITH DRIED APRICOTS	157
SCALLOPS, GAMBAS AND TRUFFLE MASH CASSOLETTES	159
GRAVLAX	161
SALMON CARPACIO WITH SALADS	163
LOBSTER WITH BUTTER	165
ROASTED LOBSTER WITH A PRAWN BUTTER	167
FLAMBÉED LANGOUSTINES	169
SPINY LOBSTER WITH VANILLA BUTTER	171
SPINY LOBSTER WITH WHISKY	173
CRAB GRATIN WITH WHISKY SCALLOPS	174
CHOCOLATE AND PEARS YULE LOG	176
PISTACHIO CHRISTMAS LOG	180
CHOCOLATE FONDANT WITH CHESTNUT CREAM	184
CHOCOLATE MARQUISE	185
CHESTNUT TIRAMISU	186
CONCLUSION	**188**

Part 1

Introduction

Holiday dinners will always present, even to the most experienced home cook, a dilemma. What to make and how to make them tops the list; and then there are considerations about how to perfectly mix and match flavors so that your guests won't be too overwhelmed. And what about child-friendly recipes? Given that the entire family usually gathers for these special occasions, will you have to sacrifice intricate gourmet goodness to make sure that the little ones have something to enjoy or vise versa?

Traditional Christmas feasts take us back to a time when a table would be brimming with turkey, roast, baked goodies, sweet treats and colorful salads. But there's an art to creating a fine holiday spread, one that this book hopes to simplify by giving you a collection of tried and tested holiday recipes that we all love and look forward to every Christmas morning.

In this book, holiday staples such as ham, turkey and roast are included of course; while non traditional alternatives that remind us of the warmth of home during the holidays are also available.

But let's say that the main attraction of your Christmas feast was not the issue and what to serve it with was. After all, when you're serving something as rich and decadent as your typical Yule-time favorites, you have to know how to temper the flavors. Which is why a selection of refreshing salads and side-dishes are available to choose from. Starting the evening right is also easier with the selection of holiday drinks, appetizers and starters that you can whip up to start your Christmas gastronomic experience right. Finally, cap off your dinner with an indulgent collection of dessert recipes that put the spotlight on holiday flavors that we all love.

Mix and match using this handy guide of recipes that are simple, easy to follow and can be made even by the most novice of home cooks.

Delicious Christmas Recipes

Drinks

Holiday Citrus Punch

Prep Time: 2 hours

Servings: 10

Ingredients:

1 (4 ounce) jar maraschino cherries, with juice

1 fluid ounce triple sec liqueur

1 (750 milliliter) bottle light rum

1 orange, sliced into rounds

1 lemon, sliced into rounds

1 (8 ounce) can pineapple chunks

1 liter carbonated water

1/2 cup white sugar

2 cups orange juice

2/3 cup lemon juice

ice

Directions:

Mix sugar, orange juice and lemon in a punch bowl. Stir until sugar is completely dissolved.

1. Pour triple sec, light rum, cherries, lemon slices and pineapple chunks.

Refrigerate for at least 2 hours and add carbonated water.

2. Add ice and mix.

Christmas Cocktail

Prep Time: 10 minutes

Servings: 2

Ingredients:

2 fluid ounces vodka

1 fluid ounce cranberry juice

1 fluid ounce triple sec (orange-flavored liqueur)

2 teaspoons fresh lime juice

1 lime wedge

2 cranberries

Directions:

1. Take a cocktail shaker and add ice, cranberry juice, vodka, triple sec and lime juice.
2. Cover and shake then pour mixture into a glass.

Garnish with a wedge of lime and cranberries.

Cinnamon Spiced Coffee

Prep Time: 5 minutes

Servings: 2-3

Ingredients:

¾ cup instant coffee granules

½ cup granulated sugar substitute

1 ½ teaspoons ground cinnamon

1 pinch salt

1 (16 ounce) container powdered non-dairy creamer

1 cup brown sugar

Directions:

1. Mix brown sugar, coffee, cinnamon and salt.
2. Mix until everything is dissolved.

Serve while hot.

Classic Holiday Eggnog

Prep Time: 15 minutes

Servings: 4

Ingredients:

4 egg whites

1 fluid ounce rum

1/4 teaspoon ground nutmeg

4 egg yolks

1 (5 ounce) can sweetened condensed milk

1 tablespoon white sugar

1 teaspoon vanilla extract

4 1/2 cups milk

Directions:

1. Beat egg yolks and pour condensed milk, vanilla, milk and sugar.
2. Take the egg whites and beat until stiff and slowly add into the milk mixture.

Pour rum into the mixture and gently stir.

3. Sprinkle with nutmeg and serve.

Clove and Cinnamon Brew

Prep Time: 15 minutes

Servings: 2

Ingredients:

1 1/3 tablespoons ground cinnamon

2 teaspoons ground cloves

1 (3 ounce) package lemon-flavored ice tea mix

2 (1.8 ounce) packages orange-flavored drink mix

Directions:

1. Mix iced tea, orange flavored drink mix, ground cloves and cinnamon in a large mason jar and shake well.
2. Stir 1 1/2 teaspoon of the mixture into 1 cup of hot water and serve.

Starters

Tomato and Basil Mozzarella Skewers

Prep Time: 30 minutes

Servings: 10-15

Ingredients:

2 tablespoons fresh basil leaves, chopped finely

1 pinch salt

1 pinch ground black pepper

20 toothpicks

20 grape tomatoes

10 ounces mozzarella cheese, cubed

2 tablespoons extra virgin olive oil

Directions:

1. Combine tomatoes, mozzarella cheese, basil, salt and pepper with olive oil in a bowl.
2. Take a toothpick and skewer a tomato and a cube of cheese. Repeat until you have gone through the rest of the ingredients.

Sausage and Cheese Balls

Prep Time: 60 minutes

Servings: 12

Ingredients:

4 cups shredded Cheddar cheese

½ cup grated Parmesan cheese

½ cup milk

3 cups biscuit baking mix

1 pound beef sausage

Directions:

1. Set oven to 350 degrees.
2. Crumble sausage into a bowl and add baking mix, cheeses, parsley and milk.

Take a teaspoon and roll into balls.

3. Place in a baking dish and bake for 25-30 minutes.

Beefy Cheese Cream Ball

Prep Time: Overnight

Servings: 10-12

Ingredients:

1 small red onion, minced

2 dashes Worcestershire sauce, or to taste

1 cup chopped walnuts

1 1/2 pack cream cheese, softened

1 package thinly sliced smoked beef, chopped

Directions:

1. Mash cream cheese, beef and Worcestershire sauce together. Mix well until completely blended.
2. Using your hands, mold into a large ball.

Place walnuts across parchment paper on a flat surface.

3. Roll ball on the nuts until completely covered.
4. Wrap tightly with Cling Wrap and refrigerate until it sets.

Baked Cheddar and Cream Cheese Dip

Prep Time: 30 minutes

Servings: 10

Ingredients:

1 (4 ounce) jar sliced pimento peppers

2 teaspoons Worcestershire sauce

1 teaspoon lemon juice

1 pinch salt

2 (8 ounce) packages cream cheese, softened

2 cups shredded Cheddar cheese

1 cup chopped green bell pepper, or to taste

1/2 large onion, chopped, or to taste

Directions:

1. Mix cream cheese and cheddar together.
2. Add bell pepper, pimento peppers and onions.
Add Worcestershire sauce, lemon juice and salt.
3. Pack mixture into a baking dish.
4. Bake in an oven set to 200 degrees for 10-15 minutes or until the top begins to bubble.
5. Allow to cool before serving.

Three Cheese Christmas Holiday Tree

Prep Time: 3-4 hours

Servings: 10

Ingredients:

2 tablespoons chopped fresh basil

2 teaspoons grated lemon peel

1/2 teaspoon minced garlic

1/4 cup chopped fresh basil

2 packs cream cheese, softened

1/2 cup shredded Stilton cheese

1/2 cup grated Parmesan cheese

1 cup chopped parsley, basil, dill and other herbs of choice

Directions:

1. Combine cream cheese, Stilton and Parmesan in a bowl.
2. Add basil, lemon zest and garlic.
Transfer mixture to a large piece of Cling Wrap and roll to create a cone shape.
3. Refrigerate until mixture is firm and sprinkle with herbs.

4. Wrap Cling Wrap around the 'tree' and place back in the refrigerator for another two hours.

Blue Cheese and Walnut Crisps

Prep Time: 2 hours

Servings: 6-8

Ingredients:

1/2 cup butter

4 ounces blue cheese

1 1/4 cups all-purpose flour

1/8 teaspoon salt

1/3 cup finely chopped walnuts

Directions:

1. Process blue cheese, flour and salt in a food processor until smooth.
2. Stir in walnuts and mix by hand.

Roll mixture and shape into a log. Wrap in Cling Wrap and refrigerate to set.

3. Once ready, set oven to 350 degrees.

4. Slice and arrange on a baking sheet and bake for 12 minute in the oven.

Pimento Finger Sandwiches

Prep Time: 20 minutes

Servings: 12-15

Ingredients:

2 (8 ounce) packages pimento cheese food

8 ounces nonfat cottage cheese

2 teaspoons sweet pickle relish (optional)

1 loaf sliced white bread, sides cut

Directions:

Combine pimento cheese, cottage cheese and pickle relish in a blender and process until mixture is smooth.

Spread mixture onto a piece of bread and top with another slice.

Cut into quarters and place on a tray.

Baked Spinach and Cheese Dip

Prep Time: 8-10 hours

Servings: 12-15

Ingredients:

1 (.4 ounce) packet dry vegetable soup mix

2 tablespoons mayonnaise

1 cup finely shredded Cheddar cheese

1/2 cup chopped walnuts

1 (10 ounce) package frozen chopped spinach, thawed and squeezed dry

2 (8 ounce) packages cream cheese, softened

1 (4 ounce) can water chestnuts, drained and chopped

Directions:

Mix cream cheese, water chestnuts, soup mix and spinach together.

Add mayonnaise and cheddar.

Form mixture into a ball and roll on walnuts.

Wrap in Cling Wrap and refrigerate overnight.

Salads And Side Dishes

Creamy Christmas Cranberry Slaw

Prep Time: 15 minutes

Servings: 4

Ingredients:

1 pound cranberries, finely ground

2 cups white sugar

1 (20 ounce) can crushed pineapple, drained

1 (8 ounce) cream cheese

1 cup chopped pecans (optional)

2 cups shredded lettuce

1 cup shredded cabbage

Directions:

1. Mash pineapple, cream cheese and pecans together.
2. Fold cranberries in.

Add shredded greens and mix well.

Red and Green Christmas Veggies

Prep Time: Overnight

Servings: 6-8

Ingredients:

1 (15 ounce) can whole kernel corn, drained

1 (15 ounce) can peas, drained

1 (15 ounce) can kidney beans, drained

1/2 cup minced red onion

1/2 cup chopped celery

1/2 cup sliced radishes

1 cup creamy salad dressing

2 tablespoons milk

Directions:

1. Mix corn, peas, beans, onions, radish and celery.
2. In a separate bowl, whisk salad dressing and milk. Pour over vegetables and toss.
3. Refrigerate overnight before serving.

Spinach and Cranberry Salad

Prep Time: 20 minutes

Servings: 4

Ingredients:

1 tablespoon butter

3/4 cup almonds, blanched and slivered

1 pound spinach, rinsed and torn into bite-size pieces

1 cup dried cranberries

2 tablespoons toasted sesame seeds

1 tablespoon poppy seeds

1/2 cup white sugar

2 teaspoons minced onion

1/4 teaspoon paprika

1/4 cup white wine vinegar

1/4 cup cider vinegar

1/2 cup vegetable oil

Directions:

1. Toast almonds in butter and set aside.
2. In a separate bowl, combine sesame seeds, poppy seeds, onion, sugar, paprika, cider vinegar, white whine vinegar and vegetable oil.

Pour over spinach and toss.

3. Add toasted almonds and cranberries.

Creamy Creole Corn

Prep Time: 20 minutes

Servings: 4

Ingredients:

1/2 teaspoon Creole-style seasoning

4 tablespoons butter

1/3 cup diced onion

1 (8 ounce) package cream cheese

1 (16 ounce) package frozen corn kernels

1 tablespoon chopped fresh parsley

1 teaspoon chopped garlic

Directions:

1. Mix parsley, garlic, corn and Creole seasoning in a saucepan.
2. Pour water in the pan, just enough to cover the ingredients and bring mixture to a boil.

Once mixture is tender, drain and set aside.

3. In a separate skillet, sauté onions in butter.
4. Add corn mixture and cream cheese.
5. Cook over low heat while stirring constantly.

Creamy Onions and Herbs

Prep Time: 30 minutes

Servings: 6-8

Ingredients:

1 teaspoon salt

2 teaspoons dried sage

2 teaspoons lemon zest

2 teaspoons lemon juice

4 tablespoons chopped fresh parsley

2 pinches paprika

24 small onions

10 fresh mushrooms, sliced

4 tablespoons butter

2 tablespoons all-purpose flour

2 cups whole milk

Directions:

1. Peel onions and boil until tender—around 30 minutes.
2. Set oven to 350 degrees.

Saute mushrooms in butter and add flour, milk, sage, salt, lemon peel and juice. Continue stirring until it thickens.

3. Add boiled onions into mix and pour mixture into a baking dish.
4. Sprinkle with herbs and bake for about 20 minutes.

Entrees

Holiday Chicken a la King

Prep Time: 30 minutes

Servings: 3

Ingredients:

1/2 cup milk

1 1/4 cups chicken broth

2 cups cooked, diced chicken breast meat

1 (4 ounce) jar sliced pimento peppers, drained

3 cups cooked white rice

1/2 cup butter

1 green bell pepper, chopped

3 ounces fresh mushrooms, sliced

1/2 cup all-purpose flour

1/2 teaspoon salt

1/4 teaspoon ground black pepper

Directions:

1. Melt butter and sauté bell pepper and mushrooms until tender.
2. Add salt and pepper and flour while stirring constantly.
Remove from heat and broth and milk.
3. Allow mixture to boil and add chicken and pimentos.
4. Stir until mixture thicken and pour over rice.

Christmas Pork Loin

Prep Time: 90 minutes

Servings: 8-12

Ingredients:

2 (16 ounce) cans whole berry cranberry sauce

1 (16 ounce) can chicken broth

2 tablespoons ground cinnamon

1 teaspoon ground nutmeg

1 teaspoon ground ginger

1 orange, zested

1 (4 pound) boneless pork loin roast

1 teaspoon whole cloves

1 apple, sliced

Directions:

1. Set oven to 400 degrees.
2. Place roast on a roasting pan and push cloves into the meat. Place apple slices over the roast.
3. Mash cranberry sauce with chicken broth, cinnamon, nutmeg and ginger.
4. Pour half of the mixture over the roast and cover with tin foil.
5. Bake in the oven for 30 minutes and add remaining sauce.
6. Bake until inside of the roast read 145 degrees at least. This should take an additional 30 minutes.
7. Use dripping as glaze for the roast.

Romano Crusted Rib Roast

Prep Time: 2 hours

Servings: 6-8

Ingredients:

2 tablespoons olive oil

1 cup plain bread crumbs

1/4 cup grated Romano cheese

1/2 cup minced fresh parsley

4 pounds beef rib roast

salt to taste

ground black pepper to taste

2 cloves garlic, chopped

2 tablespoons butter

Directions:

1. Set oven to 325 degrees.
2. Rub salt and pepper all over the rib roast.

Mix garlic, butter and olive oil in a bowl. Brush mixture onto the roast.

3. In another bowl, mix bread crumbs, parsley and cheese. Press mixture onto the meat until it is completely covered.
4. Place rib roast on a shallow baking dish and bake for about 2 hours.

Yule-time Holiday Ham

Prep Time: 8-10 hours

Servings: 6-8

Ingredients:

3 lb smoked boneless ham

1/2 tsp pepper

1 1/2 cup fruit chutney

1 cup dried apricots, chopped

1 cup onions, chopped

1 tbsp balsamic vinegar

Directions:

1. Rub ham with pepper and place inside a slow cooker.
2. Add remaining ingredients into the pot and cook on low for 6-10 hours.

Herb Crusted Salmon Patties

Prep Time: 20 minutes

Servings: 2-3

Ingredients:

1/2 cup self-rising flour

1 cup of herbs—rosemary, dill, parsley, basil, chopped finely

1 (14.75 ounce) can canned salmon

1 egg

Directions:

1. In a large bowl, mix egg, flour, herbs and salmon.
2. Mix thoroughly and form into patties.
3. Fry patties until golden brown.

Honey Glazed Holiday Ham

Prep Time: 2 and a half hours

Servings: 10-12

Ingredients:

1/3 cup honey

1/3 large orange, juiced and zested

2 tablespoons Dijon mustard

1/4 teaspoon ground cloves

1 (10 pound) fully-cooked, bone-in ham

1 1/4 cups packed dark brown sugar

1/3 cup pineapple juice

Directions:

1. Set oven to 325 degrees.
2. Place ham on a baking dish and place in the oven. Bake for 2 hours.

In a saucepan, mix pineapple juice, honey, brown sugar, orange juice and zest, Dijon and ground cloves. Let mixture boil and set aside.

3. Remove ham from oven and glaze with mixture. Place ham back in the oven and bake for an additional 45 minutes to an hour.
4. Spoon drippings over carved ham once ready to serve.

Classic Christmas Turkey

Prep Time: 5 hours

Servings: 6-8

Ingredients:

4 carrots, peeled and chopped

4 stalks celery, chopped

2 sprigs fresh thyme

1 bay leaf

1 cup dry white wine

1 (18 pound) whole turkey, neck and giblets removed

2 cups kosher salt

1/2 cup butter, melted

2 large onions, peeled and chopped

Directions:

1. Rub turkey inside and out with kosher salt.
2. Place turkey in a large stockpot and fill with cold water. Allow turkey to soak overnight.

Set oven to 350 degrees.

3. Rinse turkey mixture and pat dry.
4. Brush turkey with half the melted butter and fill turkey with onion, carrots, celery, thyme and bay leaf.
5. Roast for 3 and half to 4 hours in the oven.
6. Turn over and brush with remaining butter and bake for an additional half an hour.

Desserts

Pistachio Cream Layer Cake

Prep Time: 2 hours

Servings: 8

Ingredients:

1 (9 ounce) package chocolate wafers

10 chocolate-covered almond buttercrunch candies, crushed

1 (3.4 ounce) package instant pistachio pudding mix

2 cups cold milk

1 pint heavy cream

2 tablespoons white sugar

Directions:

1. Prepare pudding with milk as directed by package instructions and set aside. Place in the refrigerator to chill.
2. Whip sugar and cream together until stiff peaks form.

Fold a quarter of the mixture into the pudding.

3. In a baking dish, spread pudding mixture on the bottom and top with a layer of wafers. Spread cream on top of the wafers and sprinkle with crushed candy mixture.
4. Repeat until you have gone through all the ingredients.
5. Place in the refrigerator until ready to serve.

Marshmallow and Pecan Bowls

Prep Time: Overnight

Servings: 4

Ingredients:

2/3 cup chopped pecans

1 cup coarsely chopped peppermint candy canes

2 cups vanilla wafer crumbs

1 (16 ounce) container frozen whipped topping, thawed

2 cups miniature marshmallows

Directions:

1. Grease 4 ramekins and place wafer crumbs on the bottom of each.
2. In a bowl, mix whipped topping, pecans, peppermint candy and marshmallows. Divide mixture evenly over each ramekin.

Sprinkle crumbs on top and refrigerate overnight to dissolve candy.

Christmas Crispies

Prep Time: 2 hours

Servings: 8-10

Ingredients:

1 teaspoon vanilla extract

1/2 teaspoon baking soda

2 cups crispy rice cereal

1 cup cashews

2 cups white sugar

2/3 cup light corn syrup

1/2 cup water

3 tablespoons butter

Directions:

1. In a sauce pan, mix sugar, corn syrup and water. Allow mixture to boil while stirring constantly to dissolve sugar.
2. Remove from heat and add butter, vanilla and baking soda.

Add cereal and cashews and pour into a greased shallow baking sheet.

3. Allow to cool and break into pieces before serving.

Christmas Pudding Cups

Prep Time: Overnight

Servings: 8

Ingredients:

1/2 cup raisins

1/2 cup sultana raisins

1/2 cup dried currants

1/4 cup candied cherries, chopped

1/4 cup candied mixed fruit peel

1/4 cup fruit juice

1/4 cup almonds

1 teaspoon ground cinnamon

1 teaspoon freshly grated nutmeg

1/2 cup heavy whipping cream

4 1/4 cups chocolate ice cream, softened

Directions:

1. Mix fruit and fruit juice with spices. Let it stand overnight.
2. Once ready, add almonds, cream and ice cream.
Pour mixture into a deep mold or baking dish and freeze to set.
3. Remove from mold by dipping dish in hot water and inverting onto a plate.

Holiday Toffee Crunch

Prep Time: 2 hours

Servings: 8-12

Ingredients:

3 tablespoons water

1 1/2 cups chopped walnuts, divided

1 (6 ounce) package chocolate chips

1 cup butter

1 cup white sugar

1 tablespoon corn syrup

Directions:

1. Melt butter over medium heat and add corn syrup with sugar. Stir until smooth and sugar is dissolved then add water and stir.
2. Once mixture simmers, add 1 cup of walnuts and cook for 3 more minutes while stirring constantly.

Pour into a greased baking dish and allow to cool.

3. Using a double boiler, melt chocolate chips and spread on top of toffee slab.

4. Allow to cool and break into pieces once it sets.

Part 2

Introduction

Christmas is a magical time of the year when families and friends get together to celebrate. Celebrations means food, and lots of it! Families get around majestic Christmas dinner tables for meals that have been thought about and planned for days and even weeks in advance. There are so many things to do.

With Christmas Feast, I have tried to simplify your Christmas recipe preparation if you are diabetic or have a relative coming that is diabetic. You have several ideas to make ahead that will let you enjoy the holidays, knowing everything is already prepared. All you need is to warm up your dishes.

Many studies have shown that most people diagnosed with diabetes are actually ignorant about what is really happening in their bodies. It seems pretty impossible to fight off a disease if you are not fully aware of it, don't you think? People don't say that knowledge is power for no reason. In this case, knowledge about this horrible life-threatening disease will give you the power to make permanent positive changes. Knowing what you're dealing with will make you accept these next steps more willingly in order to reverse or dodge diabetes.

What is diabetes? Unfortunately, diabetes is a chronic life-long condition where your body is incapable of using the amount of glucose properly, so it keeps piling up in your blood. How and why does it happen? To make it clearer, imagine fuel. Yes, fuel. Just like your car needs fuel to get from A to B, the same way your body needs fuel to perform every task, whether it's sleeping or running a marathon. Our body gets most of the fuel from the glucose. Once the food we've eaten is converted into glucose, it travels into our body (especially the liver and muscles) and brain, through our bloodstream. Glucose cannot enter our body cells without the hormone insulin that the pancreas produces. So, when diabetes occurs and glucose is loaded in our blood, is due to the pancreas' inability to produce enough or any insulin.

There are two types of diabetes:

Type 1 Diabetes is a disease where the immune system attacks the healthy beta cells from the pancreas that produce insulin, because they are mistaken for bad invaders. This autoimmune condition causes damage to the pancreas that leads to cells' inability to create the required or in some cases any amount of insulin. This type is also called juvenile diabetes, because it mostly attacks young adults and children. It accounts for 5-10 % of the people diagnosed with diabetes. Although it is hard to reverse, the steps that this guide provide will help people with type 1 diabetes regulate their blood sugar and feel much better overall.

Type 2 Diabetes is a condition where the cells are resistant to insulin. The body keeps up for some time by creating more than enough insulin, which will eventually lead to burned out receptors' sites. Because the cells do not accept the insulin any longer, the glucose cannot be transferred to the brain and body parts, and stays in the bloodstream. This is why the blood glucose or as we call it blood sugar levels are high. Type 2 occurs in 90% of the cases.

There are many people who are under attack by this disease, but are unaware that they are diabetic. How to tell if you show signs of having diabetes? These are the most common symptoms that should ring an alarm that it's time for a medical checkup:

- Frequent urination

- Increased thirst
- Fatigue
- Unexplained weight loss
- Blurry vision
- Poor wound healing
- Extreme hunger
- Irritability
- Tingling in your feet and/or hands

For those of you who aren't diagnosed with diabetes and are reading this guide solely for educational purposes or are in pursuit of advice for someone close to you that is suffering from diabetes - it is critical that you also test yourself and determine whether you are really not confronting diabetes. It is crucial to do so, especially if you are affected by some of the diabetes' risk factors:

- You are overweight
- Have a close family member with diabetes
- Your HDL cholesterol is lower than 35 and your triglycerides level higher than 245
- Your blood pressure is higher than 140/90
- You are older than 45
- Your family background is African American, Hispanic American/Latino, Pacific Islander, Asian American or American Indian
- You had gestational diabetes during pregnancy
- Gave birth to a baby weighing more than 9 pounds
- You are physically inactive

However, even when you decide to test yourself, you should know exactly how to do it. Most doctors have been trained that when a patient wants to be tested for diabetes, they simply measure the glucose levels in their blood, 8 hours after their last meal. Do not get me wrong, this is a relevant test that clearly shows if someone has diabetes, it is just a poor indicator. Diabetes starts long before the fasting glucose plasma test confirms so. Now that we have explained how this horrible disease is created, you can only guess that the key to what has gone haywire is in fact the insulin. So, instead of measuring the sugar in your blood, which is clearly not at the root of what has gone wrong, ask your doctor for an insulin response test. Do not wait for your doctor to diagnose you with diabetes and put you on medication if you have the chance to eradicate the process. If this test results show high insulin, you WILL HAVE a chance to normalize it by following our next steps and stop diabetes from occurring.

Be Nutrition-Smart

It is scary. Receiving the news that you are affected by diabetes must definitely be one of the worst moments in your life. You know that it cannot be treated and you're labeled as diabetic for life. You have seen people struggle with this disease before and you must feel like the end of the world is coming. But it's not.

Although diabetes was known as irreversible for a long time, science has proven otherwise. You CAN reprogram your body so it can begin regulating the blood sugar again. Attacking this disease on the front of food consumption armed with properly balanced diet, you will force your body to repair the damage that diabetes has caused and make the glucose return to normal range, which will lead to its complete reversion. Your nutrition plays a major, if not the most important part when trying to fight off diabetes.

Resist the Temptation

Learning how to say NO to the juicy and delicious, but extremely unhealthy junk food is crucial for reversing diabetes. It's about time to fill your trash can with the fat-bombs lying around your house. You will also have to say goodbye to:

Sugar. When struggling with a blood sugar disease it is pretty clear that sugar is off limits. And when I say sugar, I do not mean just skipping the teaspoon in your tea or coffee cup; I also mean avoiding anything that contains refined sugar. Thinking about substituting it with raw honey? You might want to rethink this urge. Although honey or maple syrup might be slightly healthier versions - they still badly affect the glucose in your blood. Switch to stevia and say farewell to sweet food and beverages.

Grains. Wheat and other grains that contain gluten should be avoided at all times. They are packed with a huge amount of carbohydrates which can easily be broken into sugar only after a couple of minutes after they've been consumed. The intestinal inflammation that gluten causes, lead to glucose's spikes.

Conventional Cow's Milk. Dairy is amazing at balancing the sugar in your blood, but not if it comes from conventional cows. This is especially important for those who suffer from type 1 diabetes. The milk from conventional cows harms the body the same way that gluten does. Substitute it with sheep's or goat's milk and enjoy your favorite drink. Always purchase organic and raw milk.

Processed Food. Food loses most of its nutrients in the process of cooking, which can easily lead to inflammation, liver toxification and of course high levels of blood sugar. That being said, you should avoid processed and go for whole foods that will help you reverse diabetes.

You should also exclude dry fruit, soy, canola, packaged food, pretzels, butter and all kinds of frozen pre-cooked food from your diet.

Balance Your Diet

What to eat now? 'Besides the obvious why me' question, this must be the first thing that pops up into your mind on your way home from the doctor's office where you've been told the bad news. Living with this disease and being careful about the food you consume, doesn't need to make you feel deprived. Taking a healthy approach and making smart choices about nutrition doesn't have to be exhaustive. If you think that balancing your diet means eating boring and tasteless meals, you are so wrong. Once you get the hang of consuming healthy and properly balanced food, you can dig in to a variety of delightful dishes.

Make these superfoods your ultimate weapon in the kitchen and enjoy a challenging cooking that will reward you with reversed diabetes and improved overall health:

Green Vegetables are the most important food to focus on in order to reverse diabetes. Nutrient-dense, cruciferous, leafy greens and other green vegetables contribute to lower HbA1c (glycated hemoglobin) levels.

Non-Starchy Vegetables like eggplants, mushrooms, onions, peppers, garlic etc. are packed with phytochemicals and fiber and have effects on blood sugar that are almost nonexistent.

Nuts are very beneficial superfood to diabetes, as well as our general health. Besides the fact that they contribute to losing weight, they also have inflammatory properties that prevent the resistance of insulin.

Seeds like chia seeds, pumpkin seeds, flaxseed etc. are rich in fiber and omega-3 fatty acids and they lower the triglycerides and increase the good HDL cholesterol level which will help you reverse diabetes.

Legumes like lentils, chickpeas and beans are the perfect carbohydrate source. Due to their resistant starch, abundant fiber and moderate protein, the release of glucose into your bloodstream can be significantly reduced.

Fruit like kiwi, berries, melon and oranges that are low in sugar will minimize glycemic effects. Rich in antioxidants and fiber, fresh fruits also contribute to reversing diabetes.

Vinegar decreases the glucose levels in your blood. A study has shown that two tablespoons of vinegar taken before each meal lowers your blood sugar for 25 %.

Besides these power foods, make sure to include fish that is high in omega-3 fatty acids, coconut and red palm oil, grass-fed beef and raw cheese to your diet.

Another healthy diet tips that will help you reverse diabetes:

- Make sure to include at least 1 ounce of fiber per day from high fiber foods that will slow down the glucose absorption.
- Sprinkle your cooked food with herbs like parsley and turmeric that will balance your blood sugar.
- Make a rainbow-colored selection of fruit and vegetables for each daily intake.
- Never skip breakfast. Missing the most important meal of the day will raise the glucose levels in your blood for the rest of the day.

- When you crave sugar, reach for some protein-packed food instead. A hard-boiled egg perhaps, is a perfect way to charge your batteries.
- Be creative. Make new and tropical salads with leafy greens, berries and citrus fruit and enjoy that zesty deliciousness while keeping your cells sensitive to insulin.

Chapter 1: What Potential Causes and Who Usually Get Diabetes

Diabetes is a condition that is associated with too much blood glucose in your body such that the relevant mechanisms responsible for controlling these levels are unable to do that. This may be caused by your pancreas producing little or no insulin to help the cells in your body assimilate glucose or the insulin produced is inefficient (referred to as insulin resistance).

Insulin is a hormone that is secreted by the pancreas and facilitates the movement of glucose into the body's cells to be converted into energy so that you can work, play, and live your life. Glucose is usually broken down from carbohydrates and insulin helps in the absorption of glucose into the cells with the excess being stored in the liver as glycogen. High level of blood sugar level probably due to lack of adequate insulin or due to taking high carbohydrate meals that keep the sugar levels high then lead to diabetes. There are two types of diabetes: Type 1 and Type 2 diabetes.

Who Usually Gets Type 1 Diabetes?
10% of all adults struggling with diabetes have type 1 diabetes, which is treated by insulin doses on a daily basis, taken through either an insulin pump or injections. Regular physical exercise and following a healthy diet are also recommended. There is usually no specific age at which type 1 diabetes can start, but most cases report it before the age of forty, and particularly in childhood. In fact, it is the most prevalent type of diabetes in children.

As earlier indicated, insulin is a hormone that serves as a chemical messenger to facilitate the conversion of glucose to energy in your blood. It is a sort of a key that opens the door to the cells in your body. Unlocking this door allows the glucose to enter the cells to be used as fuel. In case of type 1 diabetes, your body is unable to produce insulin, the door stays closed, and glucose accumulates in the blood. The body is unable to produce energy and tries to acquire glucose from somewhere else, leading to the breakdown of protein and fat stores instead. This can result in weight loss. Since the glucose is not being used by your body, it ends up being disposed in urine. Since you cannot live with such high levels of glucose, and you need the glucose since it is the fuel that our body runs on, you then need to take insulin doses in order to open the door for the cells to access nutrients to produce energy.

Who Usually Gets Type 2 Diabetes?

In case of type 2 diabetes, the pancreas fails to produce adequate insulin or the insulin produced is not effective (insulin resistance).

In most cases, diabetes type 2 appears in people over 40 years of age, although in South Asia, where it is highly prevalent, it usually occurs from the age of twenty-five. More and more cases are being reported in young people, adolescents, and children of all ethnicities. 85 to 95% of all diabetes cases are accounted for by type 2 diabetes, which is treatable with increased physical activity and a healthy diet. Insulin and medication are also often required. The insulin produced in Type 2 diabetes cases is usually insufficient or inefficient, which means that the cells are partially unlocked, leading to a slow buildup of glucose in your blood.

With that understanding of diabetes, let us now move on to some basics of diabetes once you know you have the condition.

The ABCs Of Diabetes
Consult your health care provider on how to manage your cholesterol, blood pressure, and A1C. This can go a long way towards reducing your risk of having a stroke, heart attack, or other diabetes complications.

A1C Test
This test calculates your overall blood sugar level for the past 3 months and is different from your daily blood sugar checks.

It is important to be familiar with your blood sugar levels with time. These numbers should not get too high, as high blood sugar levels can affect your eyes, feet, kidneys, blood vessels, and heart.

For most people with diabetes, the A1C goal is less than 7. However, this varies from person to person.

Blood Pressure

This is basically the force through which blood travels across your blood vessels.

High blood pressure is strenuous on your heart, and can lead to a stroke, heart attack, as well as damage to your eyes and kidneys. For most diabetics, the blood pressure should be less than 140/90, but this varies from person to person.

Cholesterol
Cholesterol comes in two forms: HDL and LDL.

LDL is the "bad" cholesterol that can accumulate in your blood and clog the blood vessels, leading to a stroke or a heart attack. On the other hand, HDL is the "good" cholesterol that helps to get rid of the "bad" cholesterol.

Chapter 2: Diabetes Dieting Tips and What Foods to Eat

Whether you are looking to control or prevent diabetes, you can make a significant difference by adjusting your lifestyle. One of the most significant steps you can take is to lose weight. The good news is that you don't have to shed off all those extra pounds in order to start experiencing the benefits. Studies have shown that losing just about 5 to 10 percent of your overall body weight can reduce your blood sugar substantially, in addition to lowering your cholesterol and blood pressure levels. Eating healthier and losing weight can also have a significant effect on your energy levels, mood, and a general sense of wellbeing.

It is never too late to incorporate positive changes in your life, even if you are already struggling with full-blown diabetes. Being overweight is the biggest risk factor for getting diabetes, but all body fat is designed differently. If most of your weight is centered around your abdomen, your risk is higher as opposed to if the fat is in your thighs and hips. But why is the risk higher with apple-shaped people than pear-shaped people?

Most of the fat in "pears" is stored below the skin, while that in "apples" is stored around the middle, majority of it find its way into the belly, circling their liver and abdominal organs. This type of fat has been closely associated with diabetes and insulin resistance.

Let us look at different ways of controlling and improving diabetes.

1. Slow Release, High Fiber Carbs

Carbohydrates are highly influential on your blood sugar levels as compared to proteins and fats, but it is not necessary to avoid them. You only have to be careful about the types of carbohydrates you consume. It is generally wise to restrict highly refined carbohydrates such as rice, pasta, and white bread, as well as snack foods, candy, and soda. Rather, concentrate on high fiber complex carbs, otherwise referred to as slow release carbohydrates. They help to maintain normal blood sugar levels because they take a longer time to be digested, which automatically prevents your body from generating excess insulin. In addition, they provide longer lasting energy and keep you satisfied for longer.

Some of the fiber rich carbs you should consider include:

- Wild rice or brown rice
- Low sugar bran flakes
- Rolled oats or steel cut oats
- Low sugar, high fiber breakfast cereal
- Whole grain or whole wheat bread
- Whole wheat pasta
- Cauliflower, winter squash, yams, sweet potatoes
- Wild rice or brown rice

2. Simplify Glycemic Index and Easily Keep Track of Sugar Levels

The glycemic index refers to the speed with which food is converted into sugar in your body. Glycemic load, on the other hand, accounts for the amount of carbohydrate in a given food. Foods that have a high GI can spike your blood sugar significantly while those with a low GI have the least impact. There are several glycemic load and glycemic index tables available online, but you don't have to depend on food charts when trying to make wise choices. There is a simpler way to regulate the carbohydrates you take, which involves first classifying foods into 3 major categories: coal, water, and fire. It is generally better when your body has to work harder to break down food.

- Coal foods

These are rich in protein and fiber, with a low GI. They include beans, whole grains, seafood, lean meats, seeds, and nuts, in addition to "white food" substitutes such as whole-wheat pasta, whole-wheat bread, and brown rice.

- Water foods

These are free foods, which mean that they can be eaten as much as you desire. They include most types of fruit and all vegetables.

- Fire foods

These are low in protein and fiber, with a high GI. They include chips, sweets, "white foods" (most baked foods, potatoes, white bread, white pasta, and white rice), as well as many processed foods. You should limit these in your diet.

3. Control Weight With Glycemic Index

Studies have shown that the key to controlling weight lies in limiting the amount of refined carbohydrates in your diet (the "fire" or "white" foods), and concentrating on the "coal" or low GI foods that keep you feeling satisfied for longer. Foods that have a low glycemic index are digested slower, so sugar takes more time to be absorbed into your bloodstream. This subsequently reduces your chances of experiencing a spike in blood sugar levels, keeps you feeling fuller for longer and makes you less likely to overeat.

Go for whole fresh fruit as opposed to fruit juice.

*Avoid processed foods such as packaged cereal, sugary desserts, and baked foods, and instead choose whole grains, dark green leafy vegetables, fat-free low sugar yogurt, beans, and steel cut oats.

4. Wise Choices on Sugar Intake

While you don't have to eliminate sugar altogether when you are struggling with diabetes, chances are you take more sugar than you are supposed to.

If you have a sweet tooth, you'll be interested to know that it is possible to eliminate cravings and change preferences while still enjoying a small serving of your preferred dessert.

*Combine sweets with a meal, as opposed to singular snacks: Desserts and sweets can spike your blood sugar when consumed on their own. You can control your blood sugar by combining them with other healthy foods especially foods high in fiber.

*Incorporate some healthy fat in your dessert: Choosing higher fat desserts against their fat free or low-fat counterparts may seem counterintuitive, but fat puts a break on the digestive process, thus preventing blood sugar levels from spiking rapidly. However, avoid the donuts and go for healthy fats such as yogurt, ricotta cheese, peanut butter, or some nuts.

5. Alcohol Intake Levels

It can be easy to underestimate the amount of carbohydrates and calories contained in alcoholic drinks, including wine and beer. In addition, cocktails blended with juice and soda can be packed with sugar. If it is necessary to drink, do it in moderation (at most 2 drinks per day for men, and one drink for women). Combine your drink with food, and go for calorie-free drink choices. Monitor your blood glucose consistently, since alcohol can impede on insulin and diabetes medication.

Reduce the amount of juice, soda, and soft drinks you take. A certain study revealed that for every 12-ounce sugar-sweetened beverage you take every day, you increase your risk for diabetes by approximately fifteen percent. If you need a carbonation kick, go for sparkling water with a squeeze of lime or lemon, or a splash of fresh fruit juice. Also, avoid adding sweeteners and creamers to your coffee and tea beverages.

Sugar is also concealed in many fast food meals, packaged foods, and grocery store staples like ketchup, low fat meals, frozen dinners, instant mashed potatoes, margarine, pasta sauce, canned soups & vegetables, sweet drinks, cereals, and bread. Therefore, be cautious when buying food.

6. Choosing Fats

Generally, fats are either bad or good. A study that followed 27,000 people who were between the ages of 45-74 for 14 years showed that those who ate healthy fats like olive oil reduced their risk of diabetes by 25%. This shows that healthy fats are actually good for you. However, all fats are rich in calories; therefore, take them in moderation. Below are the good and unhealthy fats.

Healthy fats: These are unsaturated fats, whose sources are fish and plants, and are basically liquid at room temperature. The main sources include avocados, nuts, canola oil, and olive oil. Concentrate on omega 3 fatty acids as well, which support heart and brain health, and fight inflammation. You can find these in flaxseeds, tuna, and salmon.

Unhealthy fats: Trans fats and saturated fats are the most destructive fats. Saturated fats originate from animal products like red meat, as well as whole milk dairy products. On the other hand, trans fats (aka partially hydrogenated oils) are made by blending vegetable oils with hydrogen in order to solidify them.

7. Perfect Usage of Vinegar on Meals

Are you aware that a spoonful of vinegar can actually lower your blood sugar levels? Simply adding a tablespoon or two to your meal can help reduce the post-meal increase in blood glucose by around 40%. This is because vinegar can inhibit digestion of starch and hold it in the stomach for just a little longer; thus, reducing chances of sugar spikes. This, however, does not mean you go crazy on carbs then add vinegar.

8. Eat Regularly Within Your Schedule

As said at the beginning, you don't have to lose all your excess weight when struggling with diabetes in order to reap all the benefits. What's more, you don't have to starve yourself or obsessively count your calories. Studies have shown that eating regularly and journaling what you eat are two of the most effective strategies to lose weight. Your body is more capable of regulating your weight and blood sugar levels when you stick to a regular meal schedule. Go for moderate, but consistent portion sizes for every snack or meal.

Do not skip breakfast: Take a good breakfast in the morning to start your day off. This will provide you with enough energy to tackle the better part of the day, and ensure steady blood sugar levels.

Maintain the same calorie intake: Being in control of the number of calories you take on a daily basis can affect the consistency of your blood sugar levels. Maintain the same number of calories each day, instead of not eating much one day, and then overeating on the next.

Eat small, regular meals: People have a tendency to overeat when they are very hungry, so taking regular meals will help you keep an eye on your portions. Furthermore, you don't want instances where your blood sugar goes really low then after a meal goes up too high. When you eat regular small meals, you are able to manage your sugar levels easily.

Keeping a food diary has been shown to be highly advantageous when you are trying to lose weight as well as monitor what triggers your high blood sugar levels. This is because it enables you to identify problem areas, for example, your morning latte or afternoon snack, where there are more calories than expected. What's more, it makes you more aware of what you are eating, how much, and why, which can help you cut back on emotional eating and mindless snacking.

Chapter 3: Best Health Supplements for Diabetes

One of the main reasons why nutritional support is crucial is because diabetes is a condition that tends to waste and deplete nutrition. Hiked blood glucose levels behave like a diuretic, leading to significant loss of nutrients through the urine. As such, if you are struggling with diabetes, you are more likely to have a deficiency of vital water-soluble minerals and vitamins. Surprisingly, most professionals who specialize in diabetes do not attempt to replace the lost nutrients, and the patients end up paying the inevitable costs of nutritional deficiencies.

The second reason why it is essential to take nutritional supplements for diabetes is that increasing your nutrient intake carefully to enhance your body's ability to utilize insulin can go a long way towards maintaining healthy levels of your blood sugar. If you have diabetes, you should at least take a high-quality mineral and vitamin supplement every day.

Must Have Supplements For Reversing Diabetes

Ensure that you are getting the nutrients outlined below, besides a multivitamin. Several are incorporated into multivitamins, but sometimes not at the recommended dosages.

B-complex vitamins

Specifically, vitamins B12 and B6 support nerve health that is crucial for dealing with such conditions as diabetic neuropathy. Another vital B complex vitamin is biotin, which is necessary for growth and metabolism. Biotin also plays a role in the production and utilization of carbohydrates, fats, and protein.

Take 300mcg of biotin, 150mcg of B12, and 75mg of B6 every day.

Vitamin C

This supplement reduces sorbitol levels, the sugar that tends to accumulate and damage cells in your nerves, kidneys, and eyes. The daily-recommended dose is 1,000mg at the very least.

Vitamin D

Vitamin D stimulates genes that boost the manufacture of antimicrobial peptides referred to as cathelicidins, which terminate bacteria, viruses, and other germs. Since people with diabetes have a higher risk of developing infections due to periodontal disease and diabetic ulcers, it is important to ensure that your body has ideal levels of vitamin D. The daily-recommended dose of supplemental vitamin D is 2,000 IU at the very least.

Vitamin E

This is the best fat-soluble antioxidant for your body. It supports glucose control, and shields nerves and blood vessels from the damage of free radicals, which is fast-tracked by diabetes. In fact, high intake of supplemental vitamin E has been shown to reverse the damage caused by diabetes on the nerves, as well as protect against atherosclerosis, and diabetic cataracts. The daily-recommended dose for vitamin E is 300 IU at the very least, regardless of your health status.

However, ensure that you take the natural form of vitamin E only, which is usually listed as d-alpha-tocopheryl or d-alpha-tocopherol. You can differentiate it from synthetic vitamin E, which is usually listed as dl-alpha tocopheryl or dl-alpha-tocopherol.

Magnesium

This mineral is crucial for protein synthesis and energy production, DNA production, and cellular replication. Studies have also shown that magnesium can also help reduce insulin resistance. The daily-recommended dose is 500 to 1,000mg every day.

Vanadium

Vanadium acts as insulin in your body and helps stabilize blood sugar levels. The daily-recommended dose is 100mg.

Chromium

This trace mineral enhances the activity of insulin and helps transfer glucose into the cells, as well as other nutrients. Chromium does not facilitate the production of more insulin in your body – rather, it improves its efficiency. This mineral has also been shown to improve glucose metabolism. The daily recommended dose is 200mcg.

Berberine

This is a plant alkaloid whose target is AMPK (AMP-activated protein kinase), an ancient and very basic metabolism regulator that is present in all plants and animals. AMPK facilitates the absorption of glucose into your body's cells, reduces the production of glucose in your liver, and improves insulin sensitivity. The daily-recommended dose is 1,500mg.

Purslane

This is a plant that is generally considered to be a weed in America but enjoyed as a food in Asia and Europe. But purslane can also help control blood sugar levels. Research has shown that a patented extract of the plant can increase insulin sensitivity, slow the movement of glucose into the blood from the intestines, and enhance the uptake of glucose into the cells. The daily-recommended dose is 180mg.

Gymnema sylvestre

This is an extract of the leaves from a climbing plant that is native to the South and Central Indian forests. The leaves are packed with gymnemic acids, which can slow the transfer of glucose from the intestines into your blood. This subsequently helps maintain healthy levels of blood sugar. The daily-recommended dose is 200mg. You can also take 400mg for extra support.

Banaba leaf extract

This originated from Asia and is packed with corosolic acid, which promotes the transport of glucose into the cells, maintaining an even level of blood sugar in the process. The daily recommended dose is 3mg.

Herbs can have strong medicinal effects on your body, and interact dangerously with some drugs. If you are under any medication, consult with your doctor before embracing herbal products.

Chapter 4: Breakfast Recipes

Diabetic breakfast does not limit you to eat tasteless foods. In fact, diabetic patients can still eat pancakes, waffles and other delicious breakfast fares. Below are delicious breakfast recipes that you would never have guessed to be diabetes-friendly.

Denver Omelet

Prep time: 4 minutes

Cook time: 1 minutes

Serves: 1

Ingredients

- 2 tablespoon butter
- ¼ cup chopped onions
- ¼ cup green bell pepper, diced
- ¼ cup halved grape tomatoes

- 2 eggs
- ¼ cup chopped ham

Directions

1. Sautee the onions and bell pepper, with the butter, in a small skillet.
2. Whip the eggs and mix the ingredients in a bowl.
3. Microwave for one minute.
4. Pre-cook the peppers and onions and place in zip-lock freezer bags by portions, add the ham to the bags. Freeze. The night before making, place the peppers mix in the fridge to thaw or microwave for one minute before adding to the whipped egg to make.

Nutritional Value: Calories: 605, Total Fat: 46g, Protein: 39g, Total Carbs: 6g, Dietary Fiber: 2g, Sugar: 0g, Sodium: 380mg

Spinach and Swiss Quiche

Prep time: 19 minutes

Cook time: 29 minutes

Serves: 4

Ingredients

- 2 tablespoon butter
- 6 oz. frozen chopped spinach, drained and thawed
- 1 cup cream
- 1 cup hand-shredded swiss cheese or hand-shredded cheese
- ¼ tablespoon salt
- 1 diced white onion
- 4 eggs
- ⅛ tablespoon nutmeg
- ¼ tablespoon black pepper, ground

Directions

1. Heat the oven to 350 degrees.
2. Then spray a pie pan with your choice of cooking spray. Spray liberally as eggs may stick.
3. Cook onions in butter till glassy, then add the spinach and simmer until the water is gone.
4. Mix all of the ingredients in a bowl, including the spices.
5. Pour into the pie pan.
6. Bake for 29 minutes.
7. Cool for 9 minutes and cut into quarters.
8. Wrap a cooled slice of quiche in saran wrap, then place in a zip-lock bag. Microwave for 1 minute in two 30-second bursts.

Nutritional Value: Calories: 417, Total Fat: 37g, Protein: 15g, Total Carbs: 4g, Dietary Fiber: 1.5g, Sugar: 0g, Sodium: 209mg

Ham Rollups

Prep time: 9 minutes

Cook time: 0 minutes

Serves: 6

Ingredients

- 6 Tortilla Factory low carb whole wheat tortillas
- 8 oz. whipped cream cheese
- 6 slices ham, the rectangular kind, cut in half
- ½ cup pickle dill relish
- 2 tablespoon mayonnaise
- 2 tablespoon Dijon mustard

Directions

1. Combine cream cheese, dill relish, mustard and mayo in a bowl.

2. Lay one tortilla out on waxed paper or saran wrap.
3. Place one slice of ham on top.
4. Spread ham slices with the cream cheese mixture.
5. Roll the entire piece up.
6. Cut in half.
7. Refrigerate until serving, 1 whole tortilla is one serving, so if cut in half, is still one serving.
8. Place serving size per individual zip-lock bag.

Nutritional Value: Calories: 228, Total Fat: 18g, Protein: 18g, Total Carbs: 6g, Dietary Fiber: 7g, Sugar: 0g, Sodium: 358mg

Huevos Rancheros

Prep time: 9 minutes

Cook time: 19 minutes

Serves: 4

Ingredients

- 4 oz. cooked ground sirloin
- ½ cup Pace Salsa Verde
- 4 eggs
- 4 slices Canadian bacon
- 4 Tortilla Factory Low Carb Whole Wheat tortillas
- 4 tablespoon water
- 4 tablespoon butter

Directions

1. Melt the butter in a glass bowl.
2. Quickly whip the egg and water with the butter.

3. Microwave 1 minute.
4. Place the tortilla in the microwave for 10 seconds.
5. Layer as follows: Tortilla, Canadian bacon, ground beef, egg, salsa.
6. Place Canadian bacon, cooked sirloin, and salsa into a zip-lock bag. Freeze or refrigerate. Place the tortillas in the fridge to keep them fresh. Add the eggs, etc. when microwaving

Nutritional Value: Calories: 277, Total Fat: 17g, Protein: 20g, Total Carbs: 8g, Dietary Fiber: 13g, Sugar: 3g, Sodium: 720mg

Sausage Egg Muffins

Prep time: 10minutes

Cook time: 29 minutes

Serves: 12

Ingredients

- 12 oz. cooked sausage crumbles
- 12 eggs
- ¼ cup milk
- 2 cups cheddar cheese, sharp, hand-shredded
- ¼ tablespoon black pepper or chili pepper

Directions

1. Mix all the ingredients.
2. Pour into 12 greased muffin papers (in a pan).
3. Bake at 375 degrees for 29 minutes.

4. Cool for 4 minutes before serving.

Freezing Instructions

5. After cooling, place in zip-lock freezer bag. For the best flavor, heat in microwave or toaster oven before eating.

Nutritional Value: Calories: 200, Total Fat: 39g, Protein: 16g, Total Carbs: 2g, Dietary Fiber: 0g, Sugar: 0, Sodium: 370mg

Junior Mint Shake

Prep time: 4 minutes

Cook time: 0

Serves: 1

Ingredients

- 2 tablespoon cocoa
- 6 oz. COLD water
- ¼ cup protein powder or chocolate
- 3 drops peppermint flavoring

- ½ cup cottage cheese
- 2 packets sweetener
- 5 ice cubes

Directions

1. Mix the ingredients and emulsify by blending.
2. Blend until thick.
3. Combine dry ingredients and place in zip-lock bag. Combine cottage cheese and sweetener and refrigerate.

Nutritional Value: Calories: 200, Total Fat: 2g, Protein: 39g, Total Carbs: 7g, Dietary Fiber: 1g, Sugar: 3g, Sodium: 348mg

Chapter 5: Main Dish Recipes

Smothered Pan Seared Salmon

Prep Time: 20 Minutes

Serves: 4

Ingredients:

- 4, 4 ounces salmon fillets
- 2 tablespoons of coconut oil
- 1 tablespoon of salt
- ½ tablespoon of black pepper
- 1 tablespoon of garlic, powdered
- 1 tablespoon of onion, powdered
- 4 tablespoons of butter
- ½ cup of Greek yogurt, plain

- ½ cup of sour cream
- 2 tablespoon of extra virgin olive
- 1 tablespoon of dill, dried
- 1 lemon, fresh and juice only
- Dash of Tabasco sauce

Directions:

1. Use a medium bowl and add in the salt, black pepper, garlic, and onion. Stir well to mix. Sprinkle this mixture over the salmon fillets. Set the remaining seasoning aside.
2. Place a large skillet over medium to high heat. Add in the coconut oil and once the oil is hot enough add in the salmon fillets. Cook for 3 minutes on each side. Flip and continue to cook for another 3 minutes. Remove and set the salmon aside.
3. Add a tablespoon of butter over each salmon fillet.
4. Add the remaining seasoning, plain yogurt and sour cream into the skillet. Whisk until smooth in consistency. Cook for a further 2 to 3 minutes.
5. Remove from heat and pour the sauce over the top. Serve.

Nutritional Value: Calories: 558, Fat: 58 grams, Carbs: 3 grams, Protein: 24 grams

Keto Friendly Chili

Prep Time: 50 Minutes

Serves: 8

Ingredients:

- 3 tablespoons of extra virgin olive oil
- 1 yellow onion, chopped
- 1 green bell pepper, chopped
- 1 pound of beef, lean and ground
- ½ pound of Italian sausage, ground
- 1 tablespoon of salt
- 1 tablespoon of black pepper
- 2 tablespoons of chili, powdered
- 2 tablespoons of smoked paprika
- 1 tablespoon of cumin, ground
- 1 tablespoon of onion, powdered
- 1 tablespoon of garlic, powdered

- ¼ tablespoon of cayenne 1, 14.5 ounce can of tomatoes, diced
- 1, 6 ounces can of tomato paste

Directions:

1. Place a large soup pot over medium to high heat. Add in the extra virgin olive oil, once the oil is hot enough add in the yellow onion and green bell pepper. Stir well to mix and cook for 3 to 5 minutes or until soft.
2. Add in the beef and Italian sausage. Stir well to mix and cook for 8 to 10 minutes or until the meat is brown.
3. Add in the remaining ingredients and stir well to mix.
4. Bring the mixture to a boil. Once boiling reduce the heat to low and cover. Allow to simmer for 40 minutes.
5. Remove from heat after this time. Serve with a garnish of shredded cheddar cheese and sour cream.

Nutritional Value: Calories: 371, Fat: 31 grams, Carbs: 10 grams, Protein: 13 grams

Zucchini Casserole

Prep Time: 1 Hour

Serves: 8

Ingredients:

- 5 pieces of bacon, chopped
- 1 onion, chopped
- 2 cloves of garlic, minced
- 2 cups of zucchini, grated
- 1 cup of Colby Jack cheese, grated
- ½ cup of almond flour
- ½ cup of vegetable oil
- ¼ cup of heavy cream
- 6 eggs, large
- Dash of salt and black pepper

Directions:

1. Place a large skillet over low to medium heat. Add in the bacon and cook for 5 minutes or until browned. Transfer the bacon to a large plate lined with paper towels to drain.
2. In the skillet with the bacon fat. Add in the onion and garlic. Stir well to mix and cook for 5 minutes or until soft. Transfer the mixture into a large bowl.
3. Add in the remaining ingredients into the bowl. Whisk well to mix and pour into a large greased baking dish.
4. Top the casserole with the shredded Colby Jack cheese.
5. Place into the oven to bake for 1 hour at 350 degrees. Make sure to turn the casserole after 30 minutes of baking.
6. Remove and allow to cool for 5 minutes before serving.

Nutritional Value: Calories: 334, Fat: 30 grams, Carbs: 6 grams, Protein: 12 grams

Parmesan Halibut

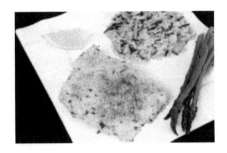

Prep Time: 18 Minutes

Serves: 6

Ingredients:

- 6 halibut fillets
- 1 stick of butter, soft
- 3 tablespoons of parmesan cheese, grated
- 1 tablespoon of panko breadcrumbs, dried
- 1 tablespoon of salt
- ½ tablespoon of black pepper
- 2 tablespoons of garlic, powdered 1 tablespoon of parsley, dried

Directions:

1. Preheat the oven to 400 degrees.
2. Add all of the ingredients except for the halibut into a large bowl. Stir well to mix.

3. Pat the halibut fillets dry with a few paper towels and place onto a large baking sheet.
4. Cover each halibut fillet with the parmesan butter mixture.
5. Place into the oven to bake for 10 to 12 minutes.
6. After this time preheat the broiler to high. Broil for 2 to 3 minutes or until golden brown.
7. Remove and serve immediately.

Nutritional Value: Calories: 330, Fat: 30 grams, Carbs: 2 grams, Protein: 13 grams

Tilapia and Broccoli

Prep time: 4 minutes

Cook time: 14 minutes

Serves: 1

Ingredients

- 6 oz. tilapia, frozen is fine
- 1 tablespoon butter

- 1 tablespoon garlic, minced or finely chopped
- 1 tablespoon of lemon pepper seasoning
- 1 cup broccoli florets, fresh or frozen, but fresh will be crisper

Directions

1. Set the pre-warmed oven for 350 degrees.
2. Place the fish in an aluminum foil packet.
3. Arrange the broccoli around the fish to make an attractive arrangement.
4. Sprinkle the lemon pepper on the fish.
5. Close the packet and seal, bake for 14 minutes.
6. Combine the garlic and butter. Set aside.
7. Remove the packet from the oven and transfer ingredients to a plate.
8. Place the butter on the fish and broccoli.
9. Place the butter and garlic into small sealed containers or zip-lock bags, Refrigerate or freeze. Cut the broccoli (if fresh) and place in zip-lock bags in the fridge. Place the lemon pepper into a small container.

Nutritional Value: Calories: 362, Total Fat: 25g, Protein: 29g, Total Carbs: 3.5g, Dietary Fiber: 3g, Sugar: 0g, Sodium: 0mg

Steak Salad with Asian Spice

Prep time: 4 minutes

Cook time: 4 minutes

Serves: 2

Ingredients

- 2 tablespoons sriracha sauce
- 1 tablespoon garlic, minced
- 1 tablespoon ginger, fresh, grated
- 1 bell pepper, yellow, cut into thin strips
- 1 bell pepper, red, cut into thin strips
- 1 tablespoon sesame oil, garlic
- 1 Splenda packet
- ½ tablespoon curry powder
- ½ tablespoon rice wine vinegar
- 8 oz. of beef sirloin, cut into strips
- 2 cups baby spinach, stemmed

- ½ head butter lettuce, torn or chopped into bite-sized pieces

Directions

1. Place the garlic, sriracha sauce, 1 tablespoon sesame oil, rice wine vinegar, and Splenda into a bowl and combine well.
2. Pour half of this mix into a zip-lock bag. Add the steak to marinade while you are preparing the salad.
3. Assemble the brightly colored salad by layering in two bowls.
4. Place the baby spinach into the bottom of the bowl. Place the butter lettuce next.
5. Mix the two peppers and place on top.
6. Remove the steak from the marinade and discard the liquid and bag.
7. Heat the sesame oil and quickly stir fry the steak until desired doneness, it should take about 3 minutes.
8. Place the steak on top of the salad.
9. Drizzle with the remaining dressing (other half of marinade mix).
10. Sprinkle sriracha sauce across the salad.
11. Combine the salad ingredients and place in a zip-lock bag in the fridge. Mix the marinade and halve into 2 zip-lock bags. Place the sriracha sauce into a small sealed container. Slice the steak and freeze in a zip-lock bag with the marinade. To prepare, mix the ingredients like the initial directions. Stir fry the marinated beef for 4 minutes to take into consideration the beef is frozen.

Nutritional Value: Calories: 350, Total Fat: 23g, Protein: 28g, Total Carbs: 7g, Dietary Fiber: 3.5, Sugar: 0, Sodium: 267mg

Hangar Steak

Prep Time: 4 Hours and 15 Minutes

Serves: 8

Ingredients:

- 2 pounds of hanger steak, cleaned and trimmed
- 1 tablespoon of salt
- 1 tablespoon of black pepper
- 1 tablespoon of garlic, granulated
- ½ cup of extra virgin olive
- 2 tablespoon of soy sauce
- 2 tablespoon of vinegar, red wine
- ½ cup of red wine
- 2 tablespoons of rosemary, fresh
- 1 stick of butter, melted

Directions:

1. Add all of the ingredients except for the hangar steak and melted butter into a large bowl. Stir well until evenly mixed.
2. Add in the hangar steak and toss to coat. Cover and set in the fridge to marinate for 4 hours.
3. After this time preheat an outdoor grill to medium heat.
4. Place the marinated steak onto the grill. Grill for 5 to 10 minutes on each side or until cooked to the desired doneness.
5. Remove from the grill and drizzle the melted butter over the steak. Serve.

Nutritional Value: Calories: 338, Fat: 26 grams, Carbs: 1 gram, Protein: 25 grams

2 tablespoons of soy sauce Italian Meatballs

Prep Time: 40 Minutes

Serves: 4

Ingredients:

- 1 pound of beef, lean and ground
- 1 tablespoon of Italian seasoning
- 1 tablespoon of garlic, granulated
- ½ tablespoon of onion, powdered
- 2 tablespoons of salt
- ½ tablespoon of black pepper
- 1 tablespoon of Worcestershire sauce
- 2 tablespoons of tomato paste
- 1 egg, large
- 2 tablespoon of flaxseed meal
- ¼ cup of Parmesan cheese, grated
- ¼ cup of mozzarella cheese, shredded

Directions:

1. Use a large bowl and add in the ground beef, Italian seasoning, garlic, onion, a dash of salt and black pepper, Worcestershire sauce and tomato paste. Stir well to mix.
2. Add the remaining ingredients into the bowl and stir well to mix.
3. Preheat the oven to 400 degrees.
4. While the oven is heating up, form the mixture into even sized meatballs. Place the meatballs onto a lightly greased baking sheet.
5. Place into the oven to bake for 20 minutes or until cooked through.
6. Remove and serve immediately with a meal of your choice.

Nutritional Value: Calories: 451, Fat: 39 grams, Carbs: 3 grams, Protein: 22 grams

Healthy Kale Chicken Caesar Salad

Prep Time: 35 Minutes

Serves: 8

Ingredients for the salad:

- 2 chicken breasts, boneless and skinless
- 4 tablespoon of extra virgin olive oil
- 2 tablespoons of salt
- ½ tablespoon of black pepper
- 1 tablespoon of garlic, powdered
- 1 bunch of kale, washed, chopped and with ribs removed

Ingredients for the salad dressing:

- 1 egg yolk, large
- 2 anchovies
- 1 lemon, fresh and juice only
- 1 tablespoon of apple cider
- ¼ cup of parmesan cheese, grated

- 2 tablespoons of parsley, fresh and chopped
- Dash of salt and black pepper
- ¼ cup of extra virgin olive oil
- 1 to 2 tablespoons of water

Directions:

1. First, preheat the oven to 375 degrees.
2. While the oven is heating up add the chicken breasts into a large bowl. Add in the extra virgin olive oil, dash of salt and black pepper and garlic. Toss well to mix.
3. Place the chicken breasts onto a large baking sheet. Place into the oven to bake for 30 minutes. Remove after this time and slice the chicken into thin strips.
4. Use a food processor and add in all of the ingredients for the salad dressing except for the oil. Blend on the highest setting until smooth in consistency. Then slowly pour in the oil while blending until the dressing is emulsified.
5. Place the kale in a large serving bowl. Add in the chicken and salad dressing. Toss well to mix. Serve immediately.

Nutritional Value: Calories: 208, Fat: 16 grams, Carbs: 8 grams, Protein: 8 grams

Oven Roasted Broccoli with Parmesan Cheese and Garlic

Prep Time: 20 Minutes

Serves: 4

Ingredients:

- 1 head of broccoli, fresh and cut into florets
- 2 cloves of garlic, minced
- ¼ cup of extra virgin olive oil
- Dash of salt and black pepper
- 8 tablespoon of parmesan cheese, grated and divided
- ½ of a lemon, fresh and juice only

Directions:

1. In a medium bowl add in the broccoli florets, garlic, extra virgin olive oil and dash of salt and black pepper.
2. Add in six tablespoons of the grated Parmesan cheese into the mixture and stir well to mix.

3. Add the seasoned broccoli onto a large baking sheet.
4. Place into the oven to roast at 400 degrees for 15 to 20 minutes.
5. Remove from the oven. Squeeze the fresh lemon juice over the top.
6. Sprinkle the remaining Parmesan cheese over the top and toss to coat. Serve.

Nutritional Value: Calories: 242, Fat: 18 grams, Carbs: 11 grams, Protein: 9 grams

Simple Salisbury Steak

Prep Time: 20 Minutes

Serves: 8

Ingredients for the steak:

- 3 pounds of beef, lean and ground
- ½ cup of panko breadcrumbs
- 2 eggs, large
- 2 tablespoons of ketchup, low in sugar
- 4 tablespoons of mustard, dried
- 8 dashes of Worcestershire sauce
- 1 tablespoon of salt
- 1 tablespoon of black pepper
- 1 tablespoon of garlic, powdered
- 1 tablespoon of onion, powdered
- 2 tablespoons of butter

- 2 tablespoons of extra virgin olive oil

Ingredients for the gravy:

- 1 onion, sliced thinly
- 4 cups of beef broth
- 2 tablespoons of ketchup, low in sugar
- 2 tablespoons of kitchen bouquet
- 8 dashes of Worcestershire sauce
- 2 tablespoons of cornstarch

Directions:

1. Use a large bowl and add in all of the ingredients for the steak except for the butter and extra virgin olive oil. Stir well to mix and form this mixture into patties.
2. Place a large saucepan over medium heat. Add in the extra virgin olive oil and butter. As soon as the butter melts add in the beef patties. Cook for 8 minutes on each side or until cooked through.
3. Remove the cooked patties from the skillet and transfer to a large plate.
4. Add the sliced onions into the skillet. Cook for 5 to 10 minutes or until soft.
5. Then add in the beef broth, low sugar ketchup, kitchen bouquet and Worcestershire sauce. Whisk until smooth in consistency.
6. Add in the cornstarch and whisk to mix. Continue to cook for an additional 2 minutes or until thick in consistency.
7. Add the cooked patties into the gravy and toss to mix.
8. Remove from heat and serve.

Nutritional Value: Calories: 519, Fat: 59 grams, Carbs: 18 grams, Protein: 29 grams

Classic Prime Rib

Prep Time: 3 Hours

Serves: 3

Ingredients for the prime rib:

- 1, 8 to 12 pounds prime rib, boneless
- ¼ cup of extra virgin olive oil
- ½ cup of salt
- 1 tablespoon of black pepper
- 2 tablespoons of garlic, granulated
- 1 tablespoon of thyme, dried
- 1 tablespoon of rosemary, dried
- 2 tablespoons of smoked paprika

Ingredients for the horseradish cream:

- 1 cup of sour cream
- ½ cup of mayonnaise
- ¼ cup of horseradish, drained
- ½ of a lemon, juice

- Dash of Tabasco sauce
- Dash of salt and black pepper

Directions:

1. Score the skin of the prime rib with a knife.
2. Drizzle the olive oil over the prime rib. Season with: garlic, thyme, rosemary, paprika and dash of salt and black pepper.
3. Then preheat the oven to 450 to 500 degrees.
4. Place the seasoned prime rib onto a large baking sheet. Place into the oven to roast for 20 minutes. After this time increase the oven to broil and broil for another 8 minutes. Reduce the temperature of the oven to 325 degrees. Roast for 1 hour and 20 minutes.
5. Remove from the oven and set aside to rest for 30 minutes. Slice and serve.

Nutritional Value: Calories: 640, Fat: 56 grams, Carbs: 2 grams, Protein: 33 grams

Chicken Chow Mein Stir Fry

Prep time: 9 minutes

Cook time: 14 minutes

Serves: 4

Ingredients

- 1/2 cup sliced onion
- 2 tablespoon Oil, sesame garlic flavored
- 4 cups shredded Bok-Choy
- 1 cup Sugar Snap Peas
- 1 cup fresh bean sprouts
- 3 stalks Celery, chopped
- 1 1/2 tablespoon minced Garlic
- 1 packet Splenda
- 1 cup Broth, chicken
- 2 tablespoon Soy Sauce
- 1 tablespoon ginger, freshly minced
- 1 tablespoon cornstarch
- 4 boneless Chicken Breasts, cooked/sliced thinly

Directions

1. Place the bok-choy, peas, celery in a skillet with 1 T garlic oil.
2. Stir fry until bok-choy is softened to liking.
3. Add remaining ingredients except for the cornstarch.
4. If too thin, stir cornstarch into ½ cup cold water. When smooth pour into skillet.
5. Bring cornstarch and chow mein to a one-minute boil. Turn off the heat source.
6. Stir sauce then for wait 4 minutes to serve, after the chow mein has thickened.
7. Freeze in covered containers. Heat for 2 minutes in the microwave before serving.

Nutritional Value: Calories: 368, Total Fat: 18g, Protein: 42g, Total Carbs: 12g, Dietary Fiber: 16g, Sugar: 6g, Sodium: 746mg

Kabobs with Peanut Curry Sauce

Prep time: 9 minutes

Cook time: 9 minutes

Serves: 4

Ingredients

- 1 cup Cream
- 4 tablespoon Curry Powder
- 1 1/2 tablespoon Cumin
- 1 1/2 tablespoon Salt
- 1 tablespoon minced garlic
- 1/3 cup Peanut Butter, sugar-free
- 2 tablespoons Lime Juice
- 3 tablespoons Water
- 1/2 small Onion, diced
- 2 tablespoons Soy Sauce
- 1 packet Splenda
- 8 oz. boneless, cooked Chicken Breast

- 8 oz. pork tenderloin

Directions

1. Blend together cream, onion, 2 tablespoons garlic, curry and cumin powder, and salt.
2. Slice the meats into 1inch pieces.
3. Place the cream sauce into a bowl and put in the chicken and tenderloin to marinate. Let it rest in sauce for 14 minutes.
4. Blend peanut butter, water, 1 tablespoon garlic, lime juice, soy sauce, and Splenda. This is your peanut dipping sauce. Remove the meats and thread on skewers. Broil or grill 4 minutes per side until meat is done.
5. Serve with dipping sauce.
6. Place the meat into zip-lock bags and freeze.
7. Place the peanut sauce and the cream sauce in the fridge in covered containers.

Nutritional Value: Calories: 320, Total Fat: 7g, Protein: 18g, Total Carbs: 18g, Dietary Fiber: 6g, Sugar: 3g, Sodium: 110mg

Alfredo with Scallop and Asparagus

Prep time: 15 Minutes

Serves: 2

Ingredients

- Snipped fresh Italian parsley
- ¼ tsp lemon-pepper seasoning
- 1 tbsp lemon juice
- 2 tbsp Parmesan cheese, shredded
- 2 tbsp low-fat cream cheese
- 1 5 oz evaporated fat-free milk
- 2 cloves minced garlic
- 2 tsp butter
- 1 lb fresh asparagus spears, trimmed
- 2 oz dried whole wheat penne pasta
- 8 oz scallops

Directions

1. Cook the pasta according to package directions.
2. Add the asparagus for the last 3 minutes of the cooking time. Drain and keep the pasta and asparagus warm.
3. In a skillet, melt butter over medium heat. Sauté the garlic and scallops and cook for 5 minutes until the scallops are golden brown. Put the scallops on the pasta mixture.
4. In the same skillet, whisk the evaporated milk and heat to medium low.
5. Add the parmesan cheese, cream cheese, lemon juice as well as the lemon-pepper seasoning. Cook until the cheeses have melted.
6. Put the sauce over the pasta mixture and toss to coat everything.
7. Garnish with parsley.

Nutritional Value: Calories: 218, Fat: 11 grams, Carbs: 9 grams, Protein: 20 grams

Chicken Piccata

Prep time: 20 Minutes

Serves: 4

Ingredients:

- 4 chicken thighs with a dash of salt and black pepper
- 4 tablespoons of extra virgin olive oil
- 6 ounces of butter, soft
- ¼ cup of white wine, dried
- ¼ cup of lemon juice, fresh
- ½ cup of chicken stock
- ¼ cup of capers, brined
- 4 tablespoons of heavy cream
- ¼ cup of parsley, fresh and chopped

Directions:

1. Season the chicken thighs with a dash of salt and black pepper.
2. Place a large saucepan over medium to high heat. Add in the extra virgin olive oil and two tablespoons of soft butter.

Once the butter begins to simmer add in the chicken thighs. Cook for 5 minutes on each side or until cooked through. Remove from the saucepan and transfer to a large plate.

3. Add the dried white wine into the saucepan and deglaze the pan.
4. Add in the fresh lemon juice, chicken stock and capers. Stir well to mix and bring the mixture to a boil. Once boiling reduces the heat to low.
5. Add the chicken back into the saucepan. Allow to simmer for 5 minutes.
6. Transfer the chicken back into a large plate.
7. Add the heavy cream and remaining butter into the saucepan. Season with a dash of salt and black pepper. Whisk to mix.
8. Pour the sauce over the chicken. Serve with a garnish of parsley.

Nutritional Value: Calories: 468, Fat: 39 grams, Carbs: 3.6 grams, Protein: 28 grams

Indian Chicken Curry

Prep Time: 2 Hours

Serves: 8

Ingredients:

- 6 chicken thighs, cut into small pieces
- 1 onion, diced
- 4 cloves of garlic, minced
- 1 tablespoon of salt
- 2 tablespoons of red curry paste
- 2 tablespoons of curry, powdered
- 2 tablespoons of soy sauce
- 5 drops of Stevia
- 3 tablespoons of cilantro, fresh, chopped and extra for garnish
- ¼ cup of extra virgin olive oil
- 3 tablespoons of coconut oil
- ½ cup of heavy cream
- 2 tablespoons of cornstarch
- 2 tablespoons of cold water

- 1 lime, fresh and juice only

Directions:

1. Use a large bowl and add in the chicken thigh pieces, onion, garlic, dash of salt, red curry paste, powdered curry, soy sauce, stevia, cilantro and extra virgin olive oil. Stir well to mix.
2. Cover the bowl and set into the fridge to marinate for 1 hour.
3. After this time place a large skillet over medium to high heat. Add in the coconut oil and once the oil is hot enough add in the marinated chicken. Cook for 8 to 10 minutes or until the chicken is cooked through.
4. Pour in the coconut milk and bring the mixture to a boil. Once boiling reduce the heat to low. Cover and cook for 30 to 40 minutes. Make sure to stir the chicken every 5 to 10 minutes.
5. Add in the heavy cream after this time and increase the heat to high. Bring the mixture to a boil.
6. While the mixture is coming to a boil add the cornstarch and water into a small bowl. Whisk to make a slurry and pour into the chicken mixture. Stir well to mix and cook for 5 minutes or until thick in consistency.
7. Add in the fresh lime juice and a dash of salt.
8. Remove from heat and serve.

Nutritional Value: Calories: 408, Fat: 32 grams, Carbs: 7 grams, Protein: 23 grams

No Bake Cheesecake

Prep Time: 6 Hours and 15 Minutes

Serves: 12

Ingredients:

- ½ cup of almond flour
- ¼ cup of butter, melted
- 16 ounces of cream cheese, soft
- ¾ cup of artificial sweetener
- ½ tablespoon of pure vanilla
- ½ tablespoon of lemon juice, fresh
- ½ tablespoon of salt

Directions:

1. Spray a muffin pan with cooking spray and line with paper muffin lines.
2. Use a large bowl and add in the almond flour and butter. Stir well until mixed. Pour this mixture into the bottom of each muffin cup. Press flat to make a crust.

3. Use a separate bowl and add in the cream cheese, artificial sweetener, pure vanilla, fresh lemon juice and dash of salt. Beat with an electric mixer until creamy in consistency. Pour this mixture over the crusts.
4. Place the muffin pan into the freezer to freeze for 2 hours.
5. Remove after this time and transfer into the fridge to thaw for 3 to 4 hours. Serve. Flank Steak Stuffed with Pancetta and Goat Cheese This is a great tasting keto friendly dish you can make for lunch or dinner.

Nutritional Value: Calories: 195, Fat: 19 grams, Carbs: 3 grams, Protein: 3 grams

Cauliflower Soup

Prep Time: 1 Hour and 45 Minutes

Serves: 4

Ingredients:

- 1 head of cauliflower, fresh
- 6 pieces of bacon, chopped
- 3 tablespoons of butter
- 1 onion, chopped
- 2 cloves of garlic, minced
- 2 tablespoons of thyme, fresh
- 3 cups of chicken stock
- 2 cups of heavy cream
- ½ cup of Parmesan cheese, grated
- Dash of salt and black pepper
- Dash of Tabasco
- ½ tablespoon of lemon juice, fresh

- 1 tablespoon of chives, chopped

Directions:

1. Place a large soup pot over low to medium heat. Add in the bacon and cook for 8 to 10 minutes or until the bacon is crispy. Remove and place the bacon onto a large plate lined with paper towels to drain.
2. Add in the butter and once the butter is melted add in the onion and garlic. Stir to mix and cook for 5 minutes or until the onion is soft.
3. Add in the fresh cauliflower, thyme and chicken stock. Stir well to mix.
4. Bring the mixture to a boil. Once boiling reduce the heat to low and add in the heavy cream. Stir well to incorporate. Cover and cook for 15 to 20 minutes or until the cauliflower is soft.
5. Remove the soup pot from heat. Pour the soup into a blender. Blend on the highest setting until smooth in consistency.
6. Pour the soup back into the pot and place back over low to medium heat.
7. Add in the fresh lemon juice, Parmesan cheese and Tabasco sauce. Whisk to mix.
8. Season with a dash of salt and black pepper.
9. Remove from heat and serve the soup with a topping of bacon and a sprinkling of chives.

Nutritional Value: Calories: 686, Fat: 62 grams, Carbs: 14 grams, Protein: 18 grams

Mulled Wine

Preparation: 15 mn
Cooking Time: 5 mn

Ingredients (Serves 12):

1.5 litre (50.75 fl oz) red wine (Bordeaux or Pinot Noir)
250 g (8.8 oz) of brown sugar
The zest of one lemon
The zest of one orange
2 cinnamon sticks
2 star anis

2 cloves
1 piece of ginger, finely sliced
A pinch of grated nutmeg

Preparation:

Mix all the ingredients in a saucepan. Bring to boil.
Turn down the heat and let simmer for 5 minutes.
Strain and serve hot in glasses.
Add a slice of orange to each glass.

Gambas « verrine »

Preparation: 15 mn
Cooking Time: 5 mn

Ingredients (Serves 6):

6 gambas (King Prawns / Langoustines / Dublin Bay Prawns)
100 g (3.5 oz) cream cheese
1 tablespoon of honey

1 tablespoon of sesame seeds
Mixed peppercorns
2 tablespoons of olive oil

Preparation:

Remove the heads of the gambas. Peel off the skin, leaving the tail on.
Roll the gambas in the sesame seeds and fry them in a little olive oil for 2 or 3 minutes until nice and golden.
Mix the cream cheese with the finely ground mixed peppercorns.
Pour a tablespoon of the prepared cream cheese in the verrines (shot glasses) and top it with gambas. Drizzle with a little bit of honey and serve immediately.

Smoked Salmon Canapés

Preparation : 10 mn
Cooking Time : 10 mn

Ingredients (Serves 6) :

12 slices of toasted or fresh baguette
12 teaspoons of crème fraîche
12 small slices of smoked salmon
Chopped chives

Lemon

Preparation :

Spread the crème fraîche on the slices of bread and top with a sliver of smoked salmon. Sprinkle with snipped chives and a drizzle of lemon juice.

Mushrooms with Foie Gras

Preparation : 15 mn
Cooking Time : 10 mn

Ingredients (Makes 6) :

250 g (8.8 oz) of mushrooms
6 slices of baguette
6 thin slices of foie gras
150 g (5.3 oz) of crème fraîche

Salt and pepper

Preparation :

In a pan, fry the mushrooms in a knob of butter. Season with salt and pepper. Add the crème fraîche and leave to thicken (3 to 4 minutes).
In the meantime, toast two slices of bread . Add a slice of foie gras and top with the hot mushroom and crème fraîche mixture. Serve immediately.

A Spoonful of Crab

Preparation : 5 mn

Ingredients (Makes 4) :

4 tasting spoons

50 g (1.75 oz) mayonnaise or cream cheese (whichever you prefer)

100 g (3.5 oz) of crab meat
20 cooked prawns

Chopped chives

Mixed peppercorns

Preparation :

In a bowl, mix the crab meat with the mayonnaise (or the cream cheese). Put equal amounts of this mixture in each spoon.

Top with 4 or 5 prawns. Sprinkle with some chopped chives and a pinch of finely ground mixed peppercorns.

Blinis with Ham and Mozzarella

Preparation : 10 mn
Cooking Time: 15 mn + 20 mn

Ingredients (Makes 8) :

For the Blinis :
1 small pot natural yogurt (125 ml / 4.25 fl oz)
1 yogurt pot measure of whole milk
2 yogurt pot measure of flour
2 eggs
1/2 teaspoon raising powder
Salt and pepper

For the topping :
400 g mozzarella
8 thin slices of Parma ham

8 basil leaves
A handful of grated cheese

Preparation :

In a bowl, mix the flour, salt and raising powder. Add the yogurt, milk and eggs. Stir well. In a hot, slightly greased pan, pour one tablespoon of the mixture.

Thinly slice the mozzarella. Top each blini with a slice of mozzarella, a slice of Parma ham and a leaf of basil.

Sprinkle a bit of cheese on each blini and put in a preheated oven at 180°C (gas mark 6 / 355°F) for 20 min. Serve immediately.

Leeks and Scallops Blinis

Preparation : 10 min
Cooking Time: 25 min

Ingredients (Makes 8) :

4 small leeks
500 g (17.65 oz) of scallops
8 small blinis (see previous recipe)
50 cl (17 fl oz) of crème fraîche
50 g (1.75 oz) of parmesan
A spring of thyme
1 finely chopped garlic clove

Olive oil

Preparation :

Preheat the oven to 220°C (gas mark 7-8 / 430°F). Fry the leeks in a pan with a tablespoon of olive oil. Sear the scallops in a pan with a drizzle of olive oil, add the thyme and garlic. Arrange the blinis on a tray. Spread some cream on each blini. Top them with the leeks and scallops. Sprinkle some parmesan on top. Put in the oven for 20 to 25 min. Serve immediately.

Pear and Foie Gras Verrine

Preparation : 15 min
Cooking Time: 10 min

Ingredients (Makes 2) :

1 pear
25 g (0.88 oz) of foie gras
20 g (0.70 oz) of butter
1 teaspoon sugar
1 teaspoon honey
A pinch of clove, nutmeg and ginger powder

Preparation :

Peel, core and dice the pear in small 1 cm cubes.
Melt the butter, add the sugar and start cooking while stirring regularly.
Sprinkle the mixed spices on top (according to your taste) and add the teaspoon of honey.
Stir every now and again and let caramelise a little. The pear dices must be slightly crunchy. It takes about 10 min to cook.
Remove from heat and let cool down.
Fill the verrine glasses.
To do so, place a layer of the diced pear in the bottom of the each glass.
Cover with a layer of foie gras shavings . Then, add another layer of diced pear. Enjoy!

Fig Chutney

Preparation : 15 min
Cooking Time: 15 min

Ingredients (Serves 4) :

5 fresh figs (7 if they are small)
1 onion
1 sprig fresh thyme
1 bay leaf
Vinegar Sherry/ Xeres
1 tablespoon honey
25 g (0.88 oz) pistachios
25 g (0.88 oz) slivered almonds
25 g (0.88 oz) pine kernel

Preparation :

Cut the figs into half and take out the flesh. Thinly slice the onion and sweat in butter. Add the fig pulp, the thyme, a tablespoon of Xeres sherry vinegar, a tablespoon of honey and the bay leaf. Cook gently for 15 mins.
Roast the pine kernels, the almonds and the pistachios in a dry pan. Leave them aside.
Finishing touch : Heat up the fig purée and blend the almonds, pine kernels and pistachios into it. Add a little cinnamon according to taste. This chutney would be perfect served with a nice cheese platter.

Goat Cheese and Fig Toast

Ingredients :
2 slices of multi-grain bread

Goat cheese

4 dry figs

2 shallots

Unflavoured tea (black, red or green tea - avoid those in the shops with artificial flavourings)

Honey

Vinegar (flavoured if possible - like raspberry, walnut, cider...)

Salt and pepper

Preparation :

Let a tea bag infuse in a cup half-filled with hot water and soak the figs in it for 20 mins.

Meanwhile, thinly slice the shallots and fry them gently in olive oil.

Then, thinly slice the figs and add them into the pan with a drizzle of honey, the salt and pepper. Then, moisten the mixture with the remaining tea and simmer over low heat until it has the consistency of a compote. Then, add a tablespoon of vinegar and remove from heat.

Spread the chutney on rather thin slices of bread. Cut the goat cheese into small dices, scatter them on top of the toasts and grill them a few minutes (if you prefer melted cheese). You can add some Provencal herbs before serving the warm toasts with a green salad!

Skewered Scallops with Bacon, Creamed Vegetables Baked in Parchment Parcels

Preparation : 30 min
Cooking Time: 10 min

Ingredients (Serves 2) :
14 scallops
7 very thin rashers of smoked streaky bacon
The white of 1 leek
3 carrots
1 small piece of fresh ginger
20 cl (6.75 fl oz) of liquid crème fraîche
A few coriander seeds
Unground pepper

FOR THE FISH SPICES MIX :
Aneth
Thyme
Rosemary

Parsley
Chives

Coriander

Preparation :

Peel, wash and grate the carrots. Wash and cut the white of the leek thinly. In parchment paper,

place half the leek, baste with one tablespoon of water and close the parcel. Make a second one and cook 4 mins in a microwave set to maximum power.
Take the parcels out of the microwave, open them and cover the leek with the carrots, baste with 2 tablespoon of liquid crème fraîche, ground coriander seeds, a little of grated ginger and some fish spices mix for each parcel. Leave aside.
In a big pan, fry the smoked streaky bacon rashers for 2 mins and drain them with absorbent paper. Be careful not to overcook it (it MUST NOT be crispy, so as to be easily handled)! Cut the bacon into 2, then roll the scallops up in the bacon. Hold it with a toothpick.
Heat up a frying pan and cook the skewers for about 2 mins. Cook the parcels again for 4 mins in a microwave set to maximum power.
Remove the skewers from the pan and put them aside. Deglaze the pan with what is left of the liquid crème fraîche. Add a twist of ground pepper.
Open the parcels, put the skewers on top and finally coat with some creamy sauce.

Scallop Cassolette

Preparation : 20 min
Cooking Time: 30 min

Ingredients (Serves 4) :
3 big onions
1 garlic clove
300 g (10.60 oz) of fresh button mushrooms
20 fresh pink prawns
400 g (14.10 oz) of scallops
Fresh parsley
Margarine to butter the cassolette dishes
SAUCE
 1/4 of a bottle of white wine
20 cl (6.75 fl oz) of light crème fraîche
 2 level tablespoon of flour

Preparation :

Thinly chop the onions and garlic and fry them in a pan.
Slice the mushrooms and fry them in another.
Fry the defrosted scallops with a drizzle of olive oil until golden brown (1 min, then turn over). Add 1 capful of whisky or Brandy to flambé them.
Leave aside and keep the cooking juices separate.
Prepare your cassolettes by slightly buttering each individual dish (which must be ovenproof).
Add in each of them: onions, mushrooms, scallops, as well as 5 prawn per dish plus chopped parsley.

Leave aside.

Make the sauce.

In a pan over gentle heat, pour the white wine, the crème fraîche and the cooking juices from the scallops.

Whisk and add the flour to thicken the mixture. Then spread the sauce over each individual cassolette and cook in the oven at 200°C (gas mark 6-7 / 392°F) for 30 mins.

Warm Oysters with Champagne Sabayon

Preparation : 20 min
Cooking Time: 10 min

Ingredients (Serves 4) :
2 dozen oysters
15 cl (5.28 fl oz) of crème fraîche
75 g of butter
15 cl (5.28 fl oz) of Champagne
4 yolks
Chives

Pepper

Preparation :

Open and remove the oysters from their shell and filter their water.
Melt the butter. Add the crème fraîche, 7 cl (2.46 fl oz) of Champagne and about 15 cl (5.28 fl oz) of filtered water. Poach the oysters in this mixture for about 10 mins. Drain them and reduce the sauce by half over gentle heat. Whisk the yolks with 2 tablespoons of Champagne. Put in a hot bain-marie and whip until thick. Add the sabayon to the reduced sauce. Add some pepper and snipped chives with the remaining Champagne. Put the oysters back in their emptied shell, coat with the sauce and broil 3 mins in the grill. Serve hot.

Oyster Tartar with Prawns

Preparation : 30 min
Cooking Time: None

Ingredients (Serves 4) :
24 oysters
12 big prawns

2 shallots

Parsley

Chives
1 lemon
1 egg
Olive oil
Capers
Worcester sauce (optional)

Preparation :

Prepare this dish as close to dinner time as possible to preserve its freshness.

Fill 2/3 of a small bowl with homemade olive oil mayonnaise. Remove the heads of the prawns and peel off the skin. Chop them up with a knife.

Chop the herbs and shallots with a mincer. Add everything to the mayonnaise, with a twist of ground pepper, 2 teaspoons of capers, the lemon juice and a dash of Worcester sauce (if you wish). Open the oysters and drain the water. Remove them from their shell and let them drain a second time. Wash the shells and drain them with their head down. Chop up the oysters with a knife and add them to the mixture. Fill the shells with the mixture.

Serve the oysters on a bed of crushed ice or coarse salt.

Scallop and Fish Terrine

Preparation : 15 min
Cooking Time: 15 to 20 min

Ingredients (Makes 6 Terrines) :
24 oysters

400 g (14.11 oz) of whiting fillet, skinned and boned
6 scallops (or 12 small ones)

10 cl (3.52 fl oz) of crème fraîche
2 eggs
3 tablespoon of chopped herbs (chives, parsley, chervil)
Salt, pepper

SAUCE :
1 teaspoon of mustard
6 tablespoon of crème fraîche
75 g (2.65 oz) of butter
Lemon juice
1 to 2 teaspoon of chives
Salt, pepper

Preparation :

Drain the raw fish fillets.
Cut into pieces and chop with a mincer. Add salt, pepper and the crème fraîche. Then, add the eggs and the herbs. Stir well.
Pour half the preparation in the silicon moulds, put the scallop

on top of it and cover with the rest of the preparation. Press down.

Cook in the oven for 20 mins at 160°C (mark 3/320°F).

Make the Sauce :
Thin down the mustard with the cream and the lemon juice. Add the butter cut into pieces, heat up without boiling and add snipped chives.
Coat the plates with the sauce and put the terrine on top of it.

Duck Terrine with Nuts

Preparation : 30 min
Cooking Time: 60 min + 120 min rest in oven + 1 night (or 24 hours) in fridge

Ingredients (Makes 8 terrines) :
2 duck breasts (300 or 350 g/ 10.58 or 12.35 oz each)
500 g (17.64 oz) pork mince
1 tablespoon flour
1 egg

1 bunch of parsley
3 shallots

2 garlic cloves
3 tablespoons olive oil
1 tablespoon Provencal herbs
2 heaped teaspoon Guérande sea salt
2 teaspoon fine ground pepper
2 teaspoon dehydrated green pepper
1 shot glass of brandy (or Armagnac)
40 g (1.41 oz) of coarsely crushed nuts
40 g (1.41 oz) of coarsely crushed pistachios
1 tablespoon candied orange peel
1 tablespoon whole pistachios
3 bay leaves

2 ½ sheets Gelatine

Preparation :

Cut the skin off each duck breast using a sharp knife. Cover the bottom of a terrine with the skins (make sure they overlap a little and cover the sides well to fit the shape of the terrine). Then, put one of the breast.
Chop the parsley, the shallots and the garlic.

Coarsely mince the second breast and mix it with the pork mince. Add the egg, the flour, the parsley-shallot-garlic mix and the olive oil. Then, add the Provencal herbs, salt and pepper. Stir. Finally, add the crushed nuts and pistachios, the green pepper, the candied orange peel cut into small pieces and the alcohol shot glass. Knead everything until there is complete homogeneity.
Put this forcemeat over the breast in the terrine. Press down. Everything must be firmly packed. Place a few bay leaves on the surface.

Close and bake in a non-preheated oven for 1 hour at 220/230°C (mark 7-8/428-446°F). Then, leave the terrine in the switched-off oven for 2 or 3 hours.
Once this period of time is over, prepare the gelatine according to the packet instructions.

Slowly drain the liquid fat out of the terrine. Replace with the gelatine, so as to cover the whole terrine.

Leave to rest one night in the fridge.

Stuffed Guinea Fowl

Preparation : 30 min
Cooking Time: 1 hour 15 min

Ingredients (Serves 4 to 6) :
1 guinea fowl (1.5 kg/52.90 oz)
100 g (3.53 oz) sausage meat
100 g (3.53 oz) fine pork mince (prepared by a butcher)
2 shallots
1 garlic glove
Olive oil
1 apple
A dozen raisins macerated in either calvados, cognac or armagnac
1 egg

Salt, pepper

Preparation :

Peel the apple and cut into small dices. Thinly slice the shallots and garlic and make them sweat in olive oil.
Add the sausage meat and fry a few minutes (don't cook it). Add the fine pork mince and mix together in the pan. Then, after the cooker is switched off, add the diced apple, the raisins, the egg and salt and pepper. Stuff the guinea fowl with this preparation. Cook in the oven for 1 hour 15 mins at 240°C (mark 8/464°F).

You can serve this dish with button or chanterelle mushrooms, green beans and mashed potatoes and celery.

Guinea Fowl Stuffed with Prunes

Preparation : 20 min
Cooking Time: 1 hour

Ingredients (Serves 4) :
1 big guinea fowl
300 g (10.58 oz) of prunes
300 g (10.58 oz) of chicken livers
Salt, pepper
1 spoon of duck fat

Preparation :

Stone the prunes. Coarsely chop both the prunes and the chicken livers with a knife.
Fry everything in a pan, in duck fat, for a few minutes and stir. Add a pinch of salt and pepper.
Stuff the guinea fowl with this mixture and close with wooden skewers. Add salt and pepper to the guinea fowl.
Cook for about 1 hour.

Quail Stuffed with Morels

Preparation : 30 min
Cooking Time: 30 min

Ingredients (Serves 4) :
8 big quails, purchased directly from the farmer if possible
200 g (7.05 oz) of leeks cut into julienne strips
200 g (7.05 oz) of celery stalk, diced
200 g (7.05 oz) of thick-cut smoked streaky bacon, diced
100 g (3.53 oz) of morels
1/2 L (17.6 fl oz) of milk
80 g (2.82 oz) of shallots

2 teaspoon of flour
A dash of brandy
2 dl (2.04 fl oz) + a few tablespoon of white wine
A few tablespoon of crème fraîche

Salt
Ground pepper
Olive oil

Preparation :

Rinse the quails with cold water and place them in a dripping pan. Add salt and pepper, baste slightly with olive oil and put in the oven at maximum heat 250°C (gas mark 9/482°F). Roast and turn over. Take them out of the oven and let them cool down. Fry the vegetables and the smoked streaky bacon with salt and pepper in a pan, moisten with a little wine and then cover and simmer for a few minutes. Stuff the quails with this mixture and leave aside. Cook the morels in milk for about 15 mins. Fry the shallots in a knob of butter, add the flour, pour 2dL (2.04 fl oz) of white wine and stir well to avoid lumps. Let simmer until it gets thick and then add the cognac. Leave 3 mins over gentle heat and then add the crème fraîche according to the liquidity of the sauce. Add the morels and keep warm. Put the quails (covered with tin foil) back in the oven (still at 250°C or gas mark 9/482°F) for about 20 mins. Serve with pasta and green salad.

Quails with Chestnuts

Preparation : 15 min
Cooking Time: 30 min

Ingredients (Serves 6) :
6 big quails
500 g (17.64 oz) of chestnuts (canned or vacuum packed)
250 g (8.82 oz) smoked bacon bits
250 g (8.82 oz) mushrooms (you can choose any- the more flavour the better, according to your budget)

3 big onions
2 x 20 cl (7.04 fl oz) of liquid crème fraîche

Preparation :

Brown the quails in a slow cooker over medium heat (it is not

necessary to use butter because quails are often a bit fatty). Turn them regularly until all sides are brown (remove the fat from time to time).
Once they are golden brown, cover and let simmer.

Meanwhile :
In a heavy-bottomed saucepan, fry the chopped onions in a little olive oil until tender.
When translucent, add the sliced mushrooms.
When the mushrooms have sweat their water, add the bacon bits.
When everything is cooked, add the chestnuts and then the crème and stir. Leave over gentle heat until the cream thickens.

Before serving :
Place the quails on the creamy mushroom and bacon bed. Let simmer together for a little while.

Pigeons with Bacon Bits and Mushrooms

Preparation : 15 min
Cooking Time: 45 min

Ingredients (Serves 4) :
4 pigeons
200 g (7.05 oz) bacon bits
2 shallots
1 bay leaf
1 garlic clove
1 tin of mushrooms (220 g)
20 cl (7.04 fl oz) white wine

1 tablespoon of thick crème fraîche

Preparation :

In a deep frying pan, fry the shallots and bacon bits.
Leave aside and brown the pigeons all over with chopped garlic.
Pour the white wine and add the bacon bits and shallots, as well as the forest mushrooms and the bay leaf.
Cover and let simmer over a medium heat for about 40 mins.
Before serving, add a tablespoon of crème fraîche.
Season with salt and pepper.

Pheasant in Champagne

Preparation : 15 min
Cooking Time: 45 min

Ingredients (Serves 4) :
1 pheasant
50g (1.76 oz) butter
2 big onions
1 bottle of Champagne

Preparation :

Preheat the oven at 190°C/374°F or gas mark 6. Fry the pheasant with the quartered onions in 50g (1.76 oz) of butter.
When the pheasant is golden brown, add the Champagne and cook for about 1 hour at 190°C/374°F or gas mark 6, depending on how big it is.

Partridge with Ceps and Muscat

Preparation : 30 min
Cooking Time: 30 min

Ingredients (Serves 4) :
4 partridges
8 thin rashers of smoked streaky bacon
1 bunch of Muscat grape
200g (7.05 oz) Ceps or forest mushrooms
8 average potatoes
2 unpeeled garlic cloves
2 shallots

1 onion

1 truffle (optional)
5 cl (1.76 fl oz) of Cognac
15 cl (5.28 fl oz) of Muscat or white wine
Salt, pepper and thyme

Preparation :

Split the partridges open and remove the bone from the chest. Place 3 Muscat grapes inside with salt, pepper and thyme sprig. Then, truss up the birds with 2 or 3 rashers of smoked streaky bacon.
Melt 50 g (1.76 oz) of butter in a slow cooker to brown the birds all over. Pour the Cognac and flambé.
Add the chopped shallots and onion and then remove from heat.

Fry the mushrooms in a spoonful of oil.
Put the slow cooker back on heat with the potatoes cut into pieces, the remaining grape and the mushrooms.
Moisten with wine and add the garlic.
Cover and let simmer 30 mins.
When ready to serve, sprinkle a few pieces of truffles.

Christmas Pot Roast

Preparation : 30 min
Cooking Time: 2 hours 30 min

Ingredients (Serves 12 to 15) :
3 kg (105.82 oz) beef to braise
2 onions
2 carrots
1.5 bottle of Burgundy red wine
1 kg (35.27 oz) cooked chestnuts
5 slice of ginger bread
Spices tied in a muslin bag : Rosemary, sage, 3 cloves, 2 bay leaves, 2 chillies cardamom seeds, 1 cinnamon stick
Salt and pepper
1 beef stock cube
2 tablespoon of vegetable oil

Preparation :

Cut the fat off the meat and dice the meat.

Peel the carrots and onion and then chop them.

Heat up the oil in a big slow cooker to fry the meat.
Remove the meat and fry the onion and carrots.
When everything turns golden brown, add the wine, the beef stock and the bag of spices, as well as the meat. Season with salt and pepper.
Cover and cook over medium heat for 2 hours.

Remove the meat again, as well as the spices, and add the chestnuts and the gingerbread and cook for 15 mins.
Mix the sauce until it gets creamy and then add the meat. Let everything heat up and serve hot.

Roast Capon

Preparation : 30 min, marinade 24 hours
Cooking Time : 2 hours 30 min

Ingredients (Serves 8) :
1 big capon
3 cloves
2 cinnamon sticks
1 bouquet garni
3 tablespoon of mustard
25 g (0.88 oz) of butter
1 garlic bulb
2 lemons
15 g (0.52 oz) ground pepper
30 g (1.06 oz) coarse salt
Salt and pepper

Preparation :

The day before, boil in 2L (70.40 fl oz) of water the cinnamon sticks, the cloves, the garlic, the sliced lemons, the mustard, the bouquet garni, the coarse salt and pepper.
Remove from heat, cover and let cool down.
Souse the capon into this stock and leave it for 24 hours in the fridge.
On the day, drain the capon and let it dry for at least 3 hours in a cool and well-ventilated place.
Cook it for 2 hours and 15 mins in a preheated oven (210°C/410°F, mark 7) on an oven rack placed above a dish.

Baste it 4 times with the marinade and turn it over.
Once the oven is turned off, leave the capon for about 20 mins under 3 layers of foil.
Skim off the dish gravy and add 10cL (3.52 fl oz) of water. Make it come to a boil and wait 8 to 10 mins. Add salt and pepper and remove from the heat. Then, incorporate the butter.
Untie the capon and place it in its whole on a warm dish. Serve with fried cherry tomatoes and the gravy in a sauce boat.

Truffled Capon Poached in Champagne

Preparation : 24 hours, 45 mins
Cooking Time : 25 mins, 2 hours

Ingredients (Serves 8) :
1 free-range capon (at least 2.5 kg or 88.20 oz)
2 tins of truffle breakings or (even better) a fresh truffle
500 g (17.64 oz) of oyster mushrooms
1 bottle of Champagne Brut
3 sprigs of parsley
Salt, pepper
50 cl (17.60 fl oz) of thick crème fraîche

Preparation :

Clean and singe the capon. Score its skin and insert the truffle breakings inside. Knead with the truffle juice, cover and marinate 24 hours in the fridge.
The day after, thoroughly drain the capon and save the juice from the marinade.
Put a spoonful of neutral oil in a heavy-bottomed saucepan and fry the capon all over for 25 to 30 mins.
Season with salt and pepper.
Add the Champagne, the juice from the marinade, the parsley and some water to cook it like a chicken-in-a-pot over medium heat until cooked through (prick to check).
Meanwhile, clean the oyster mushrooms and fry them with a little salt and pepper. Leave aside.

Fill a little saucepan with the stock and reduce over medium heat.

Add the crème fraîche, boil for a few seconds and adjust the seasoning.

Add the oyster mushrooms.

Heat up the serving dish (this is important) or use a plate-warmer. Lay the drained capon on it and coat with the oyster mushroom sauce.

Serve with boiled potatoes and steamed artichokes briefly sautéed in butter or mashed carrots with crème.

Capon in Vin de Paille

Preparation : 2 hours
Cooking Time : 1 hour 30 mins

Ingredients (Serves 8) :
1 big capon (4 kg/142 oz) with yellow fat.
500 g (17.64 oz) shallots
1 bottle of Vin de Paille or, if you like, Vin de l'Etoile (from Jura); otherwise, a bottle of Reisling
1 jar of morel mushrooms or dried morels
500 g (17.64 oz) of crème fraîche of good quality

1 bag of vacuum-packed precooked chestnuts

Preparation :

The day before, cut the capon into pieces. Tie the skeleton and the wings together, which will be cooked with the fine parts to obtain some gravy.
Fry the pieces thoroughly in a little salted.
If the capon is of good quality, the skin must be as crispy as the skin of a duck breast. Let the fat melt completely.
When all the cuts are fried, add the thinly chopped shallots (do not use a mixer) and cook until tender.
Add salt and pepper.
Add the bottle of Vin de Paille and cover and cook slowly for 1 hour 30 mins.
Let cool down and preserve in fat overnight.

The day after, remove most of the fat from the surface and leave it in a saucepan.

Fry the chestnuts in this fat. Leave aside.

Remove the capon cuts. Throw the skeleton away. Reduce the sauce and adjust the seasoning.

Crush a couple of chestnuts in the sauce to thicken it. Put the capon cuts back in the sauce and heat up gently.

Meanwhile, wash the morels (if in a jar) or let the dried morels swell in warm water for about 45 mins and wash them.

In a small copper saucepan, heat up the crème, some sauce and the morels mixed together.

Place the capon cuts on a serving dish with the chestnuts and coat with the sauce (with morels).

Turkey Stuffed with Chestnuts

Preparation : 40 mins
Cooking Time : 2 hours

Ingredients (Serves 12) :
1 turkey (3 kg/105.82 oz)
50 g (1.76 oz) butter

For the stuffing :
100 g (3.53 oz) ham

3 shallots
2 tablespoons of chopped parsley
Thyme and bay leaves
Salt, pepper
150 g (5.29 oz) sausage meat
450 g (15.87 oz) tined chestnut purée
3 cl (3.06 fl oz) Cognac

To complement :
500 g (17.64 oz) plain chestnuts

Preparation :

Dice the ham and peel the shallots. With a mixer, chop the parsley, the shallots, the thyme and fresh bay leaves with salt and pepper. Then, add the sausage meat, the diced ham, the chestnut purée and baste everything with Cognac.
Mix well and stuff the turkey. Then, bard it.

Preheat your oven to 210°C (mark 7/410°F).
Put the turkey in a dripping-pan with some butter and bake for about 2 hours in a hot oven. Baste it regularly while baking.
30 minutes before the turkey is done, cook the chestnuts in a frying pan with a little butter.
Take the turkey out of the oven and lay it on a dish with the chestnuts around it and the sauce in a sauce-boat.

Roasted Duck Breasts with Dried Apricots

Preparation : 30 mins
Cooking Time : 40 mins

Ingredients :
4 duck breasts or fillets
40 g (1.41 oz) butter
20 dried apricots
2 chicken stock cubes
Salt, pepper
Roast string

Preparation :

Preheat the oven to 210°C (gas mark 7/410°F).
Take the butter out of the fridge, so that it softens.
If needed, pluck the remaining pinfeathers off the duck breasts or fillets.
Score the fat skin of the duck fillets or breasts in the shape of a cross with a sharp knife, preferably without cutting the meat.
Brush the meat with the softened butter and season with salt and pepper.
Put 10 dried apricots on the flesh side of a duck fillet or breast and cover with a second breast or fillet. Then tie together like a roast.
Do the same thing with the second roast.
Lay them in an ovenproof dish. Add a glass of water with the stock cube crumbled up into the dish. Bake in the oven for 20

mins and baste often with the cooking juices. Turn the roasts over, bake for another 20 mins and baste again.

Wrap the roasts in foil paper and wait 10 mins before cutting them.
This dish can be served with mashed potatoes.

Scallops, Gambas and Truffle Mash Cassolettes

Preparation : 30 mins
Cooking Time : 30 mins

Ingredients (Serves 4):

For the cassolettes :
4 small, but rather deep, ovenproof dishes

8 big fresh scallops (with no coral)
12 frozen gambas
1 roll of puff pastry
1 yolk + milk
15 cl (5,28 fl oz) dry white wine

1 shallot

10 to 15 g (0.35 to 0.53 oz) butter

1 teaspoon of flour
1 or 2 tablespoon of crème fraîche
Salt and pepper

For the mash:
4 small individual ceramic dishes or Verrines (shot glasses)

3 potatoes
1 truffle (potted or fresh)
Milk
Butter

Salt and pepper

Chives + pink peppercorn to decorate

Preparation :

To prepare the mash: Boil the potatoes, peel them and blend them in a food processor. Add the butter and the milk until you obtain the desired consistency. Add the very thinly sliced truffle. Leave aside.
To prepare the cassolettes : Defrost the gambas and take their heads and their skin off. Take the coral off the scallops and slightly season each side with salt and pepper.
In a pan, melt the butter, fry the chopped shallot for 2 or 3 mins over a medium heat and then add the scallops and the gambas. Cook and stir for 7 mins over high heat (maximum 4 mins if using precooked scallops).Roll out the puff pastry. With a glass, cut 4 circles. These have to be slightly bigger than the dishes. In each dish, add 2 scallops, 4 gambas and a bit of sauce. Place the pastry lids on top and brush with the egg yolks. Bake in the oven for 10 to 15 minutes at 210°C (gas mark 7/410°F) until nice and golden.

Serve these with the mash. Sprinkle with chopped chives and crushed pink peppercorns.

Gravlax

Preparation : 20 min

Ingredients (Serves 10) :
1 salmon fillet (1.5Kg or 53 oz)

15 g (0.53 oz) of salt

1/2 cup of sugar

1/4 cup of Black pepper

4 or 5 bunches of dill

Preparation :

Cut the fish in two.

Mix all the ingredients and pour generously on the two fish.

Add the dill and put the dill over the fillet on top .

Every 12 hours, make sure to move them around and pour any juices on top. After 48 hours, take the fish out of the marinade, rinse it and remove any bones.

Now, it's ready and you can start cutting it.

To do this, you have to cut thinly each fillet vertically.

This can be served with scrambled eggs, boiled potatoes and a salad.

Salmon Carpacio with Salads

Preparation: 30 minutes
Cooking Time : 2 hours

Ingredients (Serves 4) :
600 gr (21.16 oz) Salmon fillet

Olive Oil

4 limes

2 tablespoons of pink peppercorns

Dill

3 Shallots

Preparation:

Thinly slice the salmon. In a dish, mix the olive oil and the juice of the limes.

Add the pink peppercorns and the chopped shallots.

Spread the salmon slices in a long dish.

Add a few sprigs of dill and pour the mix over.

Make sure it covers all slices.

Cover with cling film and put in the fridge. Leave to marinate for 1 to 3 hours, depending on how raw you like your fish.

Serve cold with warm blinis.

Lobster with Butter

Preparation Time : 30 minutes
Cooking Time : 20 minutes

Ingredients (Serves 4) :
4 Lobsters (500 gr/17.64 oz each)

4 filly chopped Shallots

6 tablespoons of wine vinegar

6 tablespoons of white wine

Thyme, Bay leaf

600 gr (21.16 oz) of salted butter

200 ml (7.04 fl oz) of olive oil

Preparation:

First, we need to make a Beurre Blanc. In a pan, add the shallots, the vinegar, the white wine, the thyme and the bay leaf. Leave to reduce. On a high heat, add bit by bit 300 gr (10.58 oz) of butter and whisk vigourously.

As soon as the sauce thickens and turns creamy in color, pass through a sieve and keep warm. Strain the Beurre Blanc to a fine sieve. In a dish, pour one tablespoon of olive oil and arrange the lobster around.

Add the rest of the olive oil and a few thyme leaves and cook in the oven at 200°C (gas mark 6-7 / 392°F) for 10 minutes. In a separate pan, melt 300 gr (10.58 oz) of salted butter.

Take the lobsters out of the oven. Pierce a hole in each lobster and pour the butter in each hole.

To serve, cut the lobsters in two, pour any remaining juices on top of the lobsters and serve with the Beurre Blanc.

Roasted Lobster with a Prawn Butter

Preparation Time : 30 minutes
Cooking Time : 20 minutes

Ingredients (Serves 4) :
2 lobsters of 800 gr (28.22 oz) each

6 king prawns

1 carrot

1 celery stick

1 onion

200 gr (7.05 oz) of butter

5 cl (1.76 fl oz) of vinegar

5 cl (1.76 fl oz) of white wine

1 teaspoon of Brandy

1 lemon

1 Bouquet garni

Cayenne pepper

Salt and pepper

Peppercorns

Preparation :

Peel the carrot and the onion.

Thinly chop them, along with the celery stick, and put them in a pan of boiling water. Add the Bouquet garni, a few peppercorn, the vinegar and the White wine.

Put the lobsters in the pan and cook for 15 minutes.

Leave them to cool down in the liquids.

In the meantime, peel the prawns and put them in a mixer, along with the butter, the Brandy, the Cayenne pepper and a pinch of salt and pepper. Mix until smooth.

Cut the lobsters in two.

Spread the prawn butter on the meat and put under a hot grill for 3 minutes.

Serve with a side salad and some lemon slices.

Flambéed Langoustines

Preparation Time : 10 minutes
Cooking Time : 10 minutes

Ingredients (Serves 4) :

16 langoustines

1 little fish stock

1 carrot

1 teaspoon butter

2 tablespoons tomato purée

Brandy

Tablespoon of crème fraîche

Preparation :

In a pan, bring the fish stock to a boil.

Add the langoustines and cook for about 3 minutes.

Drain them and reserve.

Peel the carrot and cut into pieces.

Melt the butter in a pan, add the carrot and leave to cook for a few minutes until soft.

Then, add the langoustines and the Brandy and flambé.

Finally, add the crème fraîche and the tomato purée.

Simmer for a few minutes and serve hot.

Spiny Lobster with Vanilla Butter

Preparing Time : 15 minutes
Cooking Time : 20 minutes

Ingredients (Serves 6) :

6 spiny lobsters (300 gr/10.58 oz each)

30 cl (10.56 fl oz) of dry white wine

10 cl (3.52 fl oz) white wine vinegar

200 gr (7.05 oz) of butter

2 tablespoons of oil

2 vanilla pods

2 limes

Preparation :

Pour the wine and the vinegar in a sauce pan.

Let it reduce on a medium heat.

Once you have 2 tablespoons of liquids left, take the saucepan off the heat and reserve. Cut the vanilla pods in two and scrape the seeds onto a plate. Cut the butter in cubes. Cut the spiny lobsters in two and preheat the oven to 250°C (gas mark 10/482°F). Pour the oil in a roasting tin and arrange lobster halves in the dish with meat side facing down. Bake in the oven for 6 minutes, turning over halfway through cooking. In a pan, add the 2 tablespoons of the reserved liquids and add the butter bit by bit. Whisk vigourously. Add the vanilla pods and salt and pepper according to taste.

When you are ready to serve, put half of a spiny lobster on a plate with the bits of the vanilla butter sauce and serve hot.

Spiny Lobster with Whisky

Preparing Time : 15 minutes
Cooking Time : 20 minutes

Ingredients (Serves 4) :

2 spiny lobsters cut in half

50 gr (1.76 oz) of butter

1 lemon

Half a cup of whisky

Preparation :

Preheat the oven to 220°C (gas mark 7/428°F). In a bowl, melt the butter, add the lemon juice and then salt and pepper to taste. Brush the lobster halves with this preparation. Put them in a roasting tin, cover with foil and bake for 8 minutes. After this time, take the lobster halves out of the oven and brush them with the remaining butter preparation. Put back in the oven for another 7 minutes. When ready to serve, pour the whisky over the lobster halves and flambé. Serve hot.

Crab Gratin with Whisky Scallops

Preparation Time : 30 minutes
Cooking Time : 30 minutes

Ingredients (Serves 6) :

2 shallots

20 gr (0.71 oz) of butter

300 gr (10.58 oz) of crab

12 scallops

2 tomatoes

Parsley

10 cl (3.52 fl oz) of dry white wine

1 tablespoon of whisky

150 gr (5.29 oz) of crème fraîche

100 gr (3.53 oz) of grated gruyère cheese

Breadcrumbs

Preparation :

Preheat the oven to 200°C (gas mark 6/392°F). Thinly chop the 2 shallots and fry them gently in the butter. Once soft, add the scallops and cook them about 1 minute on each side (or more depending on thickness). Add the whisky and then flambé. Turn off the heat, add the crab and mix well. Reserve.

With the tomatoes, you will need to make a coulis. For that, chop the tomatoes and add the parsley, half a glass of white wine, salt and pepper in a food processor. Mix until nice and smooth. When ready to bake, mix the crab, scallops and tomato mixture together and then add the crème fraîche. Mix well and put the mixture in 6 individual dishes. Sprinkle some cheese and breadcrumbs on top and bake in the oven for 15 minutes until brown.

Chocolate and Pears Yule Log

Preparation Time : 90 minutes
Cook Time : 15 minutes

Ingredients (8 servings) :

For the biscuit base:

4 eggs

110g (4 oz) sugar

120g (4.2 oz) flour

25g (0.88 oz) sliced almonds

For the chocolate mousse:

4 eggs

125 g (4.4 oz) dark chocolate

95 g (3.38 oz) crème fraîche (15 to 20%)

For the pears:

3 medium-sized pears (William/Barlett)

For the icing:

110g (3.5 oz) dark chocolate.

70 g to 115 g (2.7 to 4 oz) crème fraîche

Preparation of the Recipe :

Chocolate mousse:

Separate egg yolks from the whites and whisk the latter until stiff (5 min with an electric beater) with a pinch of salt. Break the chocolate into pieces to melt in a bowl in the microwave (1 or 2 min max power, stirring it 2 or 3 times). Add the egg yolks and stir quickly with a fork (let the melted chocolate cool a little bit if it is too hot, to avoid cooking the egg yolks). Then, add the crème fraîche and mix until a smooth ganache.

Remove 1/3 of the egg whites and fold in carefully to the chocolate preparation, gently stirring with a wooden spatula (do not "smash" the egg whites - you have to be patient and let them dissolve into the chocolate!)

Then, decant the remaining egg whites and mix until homogeneity, trying to introduce air as much as possible in each turn of the spoon. Cover with a cling film and keep refrigerated.

Biscuit base :

Separate the egg yolks from the whites and whisk the latter until stiff (5 min with an electric beater) with a pinch of salt.

Beat yolks and sugar until white and then sprinkle the flour until dough looks compact.

Add the egg whites in smalls quantities, stirring consistently (the dough ventilates and forms little by little to a creamy consistency).

Preheat the oven to 180°C (Gas mark 6/356°F).

Cover the baking tray (30x40 cm) with greaseproof paper (2 cm of thickness or more). Spread the sliced almonds and pour the cookie preparation. Put in the oven and bake 10-12 min. Small bubbles have to form on the surface to indicate that the biscuit base is cooked- do not let brown!
Let the biscuit base cool on the baking tray.

Mounting the Yule log:

Line a cake tin with cling film, providing for 10 cm or more to each side. Take out the chocolate mousse from the refrigerator. Peel and seed the pears. Then, cut them into thin slices. With a knife, cut the biscuit base in 3 rectangles (the size of a regular cake tin). Keep the left over, as it will be used to decorate.

Place the first rectangle at the bottom of the cake tin.

Spread 2 big spoons of chocolate mousse on the biscuit base, sprinkle with the almonds and arrange two rows of pears strips, well tightened.
Cover with chocolate mousse (same quantity). Then, put the second rectangle, pressing softly to compact the low level. Repeat the process for the second level and end with the third rectangle of the biscuit base.
Fold the edges of the cling film and place in the refrigerator for the night (or at least 3hours).

Icing and decoration:

For the icing, break the chocolate into pieces and melt in a bowl in the microwave. Let it cool before adding the crème fraîche.

Turn the Yule log out of the mould onto a service plate. With a spatula or a large knife, cover the Yule log with an icing layer and then streak the surface with a fork. Finally, decorate the cake! And now, set your imagination free: Meringue mushrooms, icing sugar, nuts and dried fruits (eventually covered with dark or white chocolate), chocolate rose petals, marzipan figurines...The possibilities are unlimited!

Conserve the Yule log in the refrigerator until the last moment.

Pistachio Christmas Log

Preparation Time : 60 minutes
Cooking Time : 20 minutes

Ingredients (Serves 6):

For the biscuit:

4 eggs + 2 egg yolks

110 g (3.88 oz) of sugar

60 g (2.12 oz) of cornflour + 60 g (2.12 oz) of flour

20 g (0.71 oz) of butter

1 pinch of salt

For the syrup:

100 g (3.53 oz) of sugar

10 cl (3.52 fl oz) of water

5 cl (1.76 fl oz) of kirsch

For the filling:

50 cl (17.60 fl oz) of milk

1 vanilla pod

6 egg yolks

120 g (4.23 oz) of sugar

20 g (0.71 oz) of Maïzena

20 g (0.71 oz) of flour

200 g (7.05 oz) of crème pâtissière

100 g (3.53 oz) of pistachio paste

1 tablespoon of kirsch

For the decoration:

1 tablespoon of bitter cocoa

Sugar or chocolate figures

Preparation :

Preheat the oven to 200°C (Gas mark 6/392°F). Spread greaseproof paper on baking sheet. Mix the flour, the cornflour and the salt.

Separate the egg yolks from the whites. Put the yolks in a bowl and 2/3 of the sugar. Mix well until the mixture triples in volume.

Whisk the egg until firm and then add the rest of the sugar.

Add a spoon of egg white to the egg yolk mixture and mix well. Then, add a spoon of the flour mixture and mix well. Repeat this until there is no egg white or flour mixture left. Once your mixture is nice and smooth, you can pour it onto the prepared baking sheet. Bake for 10 minutes.

When cooked, take out of the oven and turn upside down onto a wet cloth. Roll it carefully and leave it wrapped in the wet cloth. Leave it to cool on a grid. Now, you can prepare the filling.

Pour the milk in a pan. Cut the vanilla pod in two. Scrape out the seeds and put them, along with the vanilla pods, into the milk. Bring to a boil and turn off the heat. In a bowl, beat the egg yolks with the sugar and then add the cornflour and flour. Take out the vanilla pods from the milk and pour the milk over the egg yolk mixture. Make sure to whisk well; otherwise, the eggs might scramble. Put this mixture back into the pan on a low heat until it thickens. You will need to stir it well to avoid splitting of the mixture.

Once the mixture is very nice and thick, put it in a bowl and add the kirsch and pistachio paste. Mix well and leave to cool down. In a food processor, mix the butter at very high speed until frothy. Then, progressively add the crème pâtissiére. Mix it for another 1 or 2 minutes until the mixture is light and frothy. Reserve. You now need to prepare the syrup. In a pan, boil the sugar and the water for one minute. Leave it to cool down for 20 minutes and add the kirsch.

At this stage, we need to put the log together. Unroll the biscuit base very carefully and, with a brush, brush the syrup on the cake. Spread half the crème pâtissière on the biscuit and roll carefully. Place the log on a long dish and cut the ends on a slant. Cover the surface of the log with the remaining cream. Run a fork through the cream to create a streak pattern.

Put the log into the fridge and take out 20 minutes before serving. To decorate, you can lightly dust the log with cocoa powder and sugar figures.

Chocolate Fondant with Chestnut Cream

Preparing Time : 10 minutes
Cooking Time : 20-30 minutes

Ingredients (Serves 6-8):
500 g (17.64 oz) of sweet chestnut purée

100 g (3.53 oz) of dark chocolate (61 or 65% of cocoa powder)

3 eggs

100 g (3.53 oz) of butter + 10 g for the mould

Preparation :

Preheat the oven to 200°C (Gas mark 6/392°F). Melt the chocolate and the butter, either in the microwave or in a bowl over a sauce pan of boiling water. Add the chestnut purée and mix well. In a separate bowl, beat the eggs and then add to the chestnut mix, whisking well. Butter a cake tin and pour the mixture into it. Bake for 30 to 40 minutes.

Chocolate Marquise

Ingredients (Serves 12):
500g (17.64 oz) of chocolate

250 g (8.89 oz) of butter

120g (4.23 oz) of sugar

15 g (0.53 oz) of instant coffee

400 g (14.11 oz) of liquid cream

6 egg yolks

Preparation:

Put a bowl over a pan of boiling water. Add the butter, the chocolate and the coffee into the bowl. In a separate bowl, whisk the eggs and the sugar until thick. Pour the chocolate mixture over the eggs, mix well and then add the cream. Take 12 ramequins and pour the mixture into each ramequin. Place in the fridge for 4 hours, minimum. Serve cold.

Chestnut Tiramisu

Preparation Time : 20 minutes

Ingredients :
200 g (7.05 oz) of iced chestnuts broken into pieces

12 iced chestnuts

100 g (3.53 oz) of dark chocolate curls

250 g (8.82 oz) of mascarpone

250 g (8,82 oz) of chestnut purée

50 g (1.76 oz) of liquid cream

12 lady fingers

20 cl (7.04 fl oz) of strong cold coffee

2 tablespoons of vanilla sugar

2 tablespoons icing sugar

2 tablespoons chestnut liqueur (optional)

Preparation :

In a bowl, mix the mascarpone, the vanilla sugar and the chestnut purée. Add the chestnut pieces and mix well. Mix the cream until it is firm, while adding the sugar. Fold in the cream into the mascarpone mixture and put into the fridge for an hour. Next, you will need to wet each lady finger with the coffee and liqueur (if you're using it). Arrange them in a dish and pour the mascarpone mixture on top of it. Place into the fridge for 12 hours. When ready to serve, decorate with iced chestnuts and some grated chocolate curls.

Conclusion

Now that we know diet can reverse diabetes, as well as heart disease and cancer, let's look at the various aspects of how to eat a healthy diet. It can be quite easy to get all the nutrients you need if you just know what nutrients your body requires and where to get them. You can also feel full, satisfied, and more energetic on this eating plan, if you are eating the right quality foods. A healthy diet is straightforward if you follow these 10 basic principles.

1. Eat high-quality, nutrient-dense foods. The body becomes much cleaner and more vibrant if it is getting the best variety of nutrients. The body also becomes more aware of problems. Your taste buds become cleaner and more discerning.

Many people just need to add some nutrient-dense, concentrated food to their diet to feel satisfied on a deep cellular level. The lack of nutrients in our food may be because soils have become depleted and food just isn't as nutrient-dense as it was a hundred years ago. Studies have shown a decrease of anywhere from 40–80 percent of nutrients in food today, as compared to food in 1914. Everyone should eat nutrient-dense foods with more minerals, and fermented probiotic-rich foods.

Nourishing our bodies should be a major reason we eat food in the first place. What we consume becomes our blood, cells, skin, and hair. Our well-being depends on the quality of our food.

2. Eat organic and non-GMO foods. Because what we eat becomes our blood and cells, I recommend buying organic whenever possible. If we eat foods that have poisons on them,

or put into them by genetically modifying seeds, then we ingest poison.

Moreover, the chemical fertilizers used on GMO and non-organic foods destroy many vital nutrients in the soil which therefore do not make it into our food. These nutrients are necessary to our body's health and well-being.

3. Avoid processed foods. Choose unprocessed foods so you aren't ingesting MSG, potassium bromates, aspartame, wood pulp, artificial dyes, chemicals, and other additives the FDA allows in food. Many of us grew up thinking additives are normal to ingest, but our bodies were not made to assimilate chemicals and preservatives.

Whole, real food that has been grown, harvested, and stored in a safe and healthy way is what we are meant to have as nourishment for our body. Most processed, refined foods have had the fiber and nutrients removed, leaving these foods empty of the very elements we need for optimum health.

4. Eat more raw, whole foods. Eating organic, live, fresh, vine-ripened or tree-ripened whole food can feed the body on deeper cellular level than cooked or processed foods. Foods ripened on the vine or tree have salvestrols in them that have cancer-fighting properties.

Organic, unprocessed foods have nutrients like sulfur and chromium in them. These natural nutrients are critical to having a healthy body. Cooking, storing, or processing whole, raw foods can destroy some of the vital nutrients in them.

5. Eat a varied diet. Because our bodies can become allergic to anything we consume too frequently (no matter how healthy it

is), avoid eating any ingredient every day. Avoid eating any one particular food every day on a continual basis. I recommend eating a variety of fresh seasonal vegetables and fruits regularly.

6. Eat whole, sprouted and gluten-free grains. When eating pasta, bread, crackers, and chips, consume only whole, sprouted grains. Avoid corn and wheat, especially genetically modified varieties. If you want to lose weight, cut out corn and wheat. Gluten-free and sprouted grains are preferable.

7. Cut out sugar or consume as little as possible. Do not use fake sugar substitutes in any way, shape, or form. Stevia, dates, xylitol, pure organic maple syrup, and pure unfiltered raw organic honey are my top choices for sweeteners, if you choose to use any at all.

8. Make sure you are not low in any nutrients. Be certain to get enough protein each day, and a variety of proteins, so you get the right amino acid complex combinations. Ensure that all the B vitamins, especially B12, are in your diet and absorbed well. Iodine, iron, calcium, zinc, Vitamin D, sulfur, chromium, and magnesium are all important nutrients and should not be overlooked.

9. Consume only good fats like pure, organic, extra-virgin coconut oil or pure, high-quality extra-virgin olive oil. Make sure you get enough of the essential fatty acids—omega-3, in particular—every day. Avoid all trans fats and vegetable oils with cottonseed oil or canola oil in them.

10. Chew food thoroughly to aid digestion and avoid drinking beverages, particularly cold beverages, when having your meal. Avoid drinking beverages with your meals, because they water

down and dilute your digestive juices. This makes it harder for the body to digest the food you are consuming.

CPSIA information can be obtained
at www.ICGtesting.com
Printed in the USA
BVHW032249161122
652182BV00002B/7